A Gentle

&

Quiet Spirit

BY VIRGINIA LEFLER

A Gentle

&

Quiet Spirit

BY VIRGINIA LEFLER

SILVERDAY PRESS

FOR UP-TO-DATE INFORMATION ABOUT SILVERDAY PRESS OR TO OBTAIN
MORE INFORMATION ABOUT THIS BOOK, VISIT

WWW.SILVERDAYPRESS.COM

A Gentle & Quiet Spirit — *Revised Edition*

Second Printing

Published by Silverday Press — www.SilverdayPress.com

Printed in the United States of America

Library of Congress Control Number: 2006922528

ISBN 13: 978-0-9729903-1-8

Praise For
A Gentle & Quiet Spirit

You have given me complete direction, encouraging hope and continual refreshment by sharing your "gentle and quiet spirit." This book is a "must read" again, again, and again!

— Janet Mansfield, Naperville, IL

I just wanted to say thank you so much for writing such a great book and for taking the time to share real examples from your own life and others. This book has greatly helped me to gain deeper convictions on what it really means to respect my husband and it truly has helped me feel so much closer to him. I am also much more in touch with my fears and the reasons that I disrespect. Thanks again for this wonderful book, which I am re-reading several times and sharing with others in my church.

— Vivien Macdonald, Silver Spring, MD

I began this book as a review for 5 Loaves and 2 Fish Bookstore and ended up being convicted mightily within the first few pages. God has such a clever way of playing "Gotcha!" Ms. Lefler takes the scripture 1 Peter 3:1-6, about a woman with a pure, gentle and submissive spirit being of great worth to God and analyzes it word by word. She labels it a "new perspective" and, oh my, it is! I thought I knew all the things the bible had to say about this subject and she takes it to a whole new level using the Greek word meanings to clarify the concept. I would strongly recommend this book for all women of all ages!

— M. E. Knudson, Wausau, WI

Thank you so much for writing this book. I have really enjoyed it and am learning a great deal. Many of my friends and I agree that this is a book to be read again and again as an aid in a lifetime of growth as a woman of God. Thanks.

— Kristen Lamb, Boston, MA

Even after being married 37 years, I found the book *A Gentle & Quiet Spirit* very inspirational and challenging to my own life. Thank you, Virginia, for the help and training your book will give us in becoming better women of God.

— Patsy Harris, Chicago, IL

This is the best book. I should have had this to read before I got married or at least pretty quick into my marriage. My husband would have had it so much better, and I would have been a lot happier.

— Rosemary Stepp, Colorado City, TX

Wow—this tiny book (141 pages) packs a powerful punch! The author, an elder's wife, uses Scripture, personal examples, and worksheets to help readers see the true condition of their spirits. She also teaches the meanings behind the words of several key Bible passages as they apply to our relationships with others so that we can apply those passages properly. Although this book is very helpful in dealing with the marriage relationship, I find it to be convicting as I examine my relationships with other women, as well. More than once, the teachings it presents have stopped me from reacting to a situation and making it worse! Ms. Lefler does a great job of not being preachy or condescending; she simply comes across as a friend who cares and wants to help you have a spirit that is "of great worth to God."

— Amazon.com Reader

Virginia is completely vulnerable in the candor of her personal examples, completely practical in addressing the issues and attitudes faced by most wives, and completely spiritual in her solutions from the Bible. I needed this book; I think every Christian wife does!

— Linda Brumley, Seattle, WA

Virginia has provided us with spiritual and practical guidance to help us fulfill our God-given role. This journey has been life-changing for me, and I believe it will be for all who read this book.

— Kelly Cochrane, Little Rock, AR

CONTENTS

Romeo & Juliet – Without the Poison

In 1972 I was twenty years old and my boyfriend, Jim, was twenty-four. We had met on a work assignment at the Nebraska Center for Continuing Education. Little did we know how appropriately "Continuing Education" would describe our relationship through the years.

The women's liberation movement was in full swing. I wasn't ready to burn my bra, but some of their ideas sounded reasonable to me. Jim and I were planning to get married. I wanted a modern marriage – everything should be fair. I was not going to be a rug to my husband, nor would I use the word "obey" in my marriage vows. Jim and I were married in September of that year.

Our first year of marriage was great. We bought our first house that year and were still able to save for a rainy day. We regularly attended church services and Bible classes. During the first years of our marriage, Jim was my best friend.

Our first son was born during our fifth year of marriage, and two years later our second son was born. As our responsibilities mounted and life became more demanding, I felt less and less "in love" with my husband. Instead of growing closer, we became more distant from each other. On the outside we looked like we had a good marriage. We built a beautiful new home and loved our two adorable sons. We enjoyed many activities with our friends and family. But there was an ongoing conflict in our relationship that we didn't know how to resolve.

I still thought a modern marriage was what I wanted. I wanted to be a good wife to Jim, but I was more apt to look for advice in the *Ladies' Home Journal* than the Bible. I thought the purpose of the Bible was to teach religious doctrine. I had no idea that the scriptures held the key to an intimate and enjoyable relationship with my husband. Besides, both Jesus and Paul were single, so what could they say that would help? That ruled out a big chunk of the Bible.

The conflicts continued. When I read about the fruits of the Spirit – love, joy and peace – I was closer to empty than full, especially in my marriage. My marriage did not reflect the righteousness that I read about in the scriptures. Then, thankfully, after eleven years of marriage, we learned what it meant to be disciples of Jesus. I began reading the Bible with a new purpose. I even found that Jesus and Paul had some profound things to say about marriage.

Had you known me then, you would not have described me as gentle and quiet. I don't remember the first time I read 1 Peter 3:1-6, but I do remember some of my earliest thoughts as a young wife about it: "Why didn't God make me like Melanie in *Gone With The Wind* – meek, soft spoken and proper? Why would God want me to be a certain way and then put such a different spirit within me?" Was this just bad luck of the draw – like not getting straight teeth? At least for that I could go to the orthodontist.

I must say that my marriage has been an adventure. There has been a driving force in me to find that marital bliss, which I have always described to my girlfriends as Romeo and Juliet – without the poison. I've now been married over thirty years. I have enjoyed many years as a disciple of Jesus and have seen God help Jim and I grow much closer in our marriage. God has blessed us in our marriage in so many ways.

After Jim became an elder in the church, we occasionally taught marriage classes, sharing what we had learned. As we were trying to help other married couples, we realized that there was a plateau that we had never been able to go beyond in our own marriage. It was a frustration to both of us. When we couldn't seem to make progress in this area, we would focus on other things such as our children, work or ministry. But we would eventually find ourselves back at this same point of conflict. We were there again, and we had lost our happy stride. We got with another couple one night to discuss the conflicts we were having and get their input. As we described and discussed what was happening, they told us that it was time to grow again.

During that time I had been praying that God would help me grow more spiritually that year than any other year since becoming a disciple. I had experienced a lot of spiritual growth during my first years as a disciple, but it had been quite some time since I had approached the scriptures or my prayer times with an emphasis on my personal growth. I had no idea how God was going to answer my prayer for much growth, but God saw plenty of areas for me to work on. He was about to help me make some deep character changes. It was like God had turned on a neon sign that my marriage was the place for me to grow. So I began an in-depth Bible study about marriage.

As I discussed what I was studying with other women, I discovered that many Christian women today face a dilemma in regard to the biblical teaching about a gentle and quiet spirit. They want to please God, yet they think of these qualities as unappealing or unattainable. Some said that they see "gentle" and "quiet" as weak or passive qualities. Others said that they think these qualities are unattainable because of their own outgoing personality.

So what's a modern Christian woman to do? Well, take heart because I have good news. The truth is that these are amazing qualities, both appealing and attainable. We can clear up these misunderstandings by looking at the original Greek text. Furthermore, many women are surprised to find out that "gentle" and "quiet" are not feminine qualities. These qualities helped Jesus live a powerful, righteous life. So get ready to build your spiritual muscles!

I share these things with you as sisterly advice – not as a professional counselor. It is my hope that these scriptures will bless your life as much as they have mine. Most of this book is written from a wife's perspective, but a gentle and quiet spirit is for all women whether you are married or single.

I encourage you to use the journal pages at the end of each chapter to make notes, write prayers and journal your progress. It will be a treasure for you to go back to when you need encouragement.

MORE RESOURCES: I invite you to listen to a 35-minute introductory lesson that addresses the challenges we face in becoming women with a gentle and quiet spirit. This free audio lesson and other resources are available at www.SilverdayPress.com.

May God bless you as you grow in a gentle and quiet spirit!

Virginia Lefler

● – ●

Worksheet 1 - Definitions

1. Before you begin this study, write your definitions of "gentle" and "quiet."

- Chapter 1 -

A New Perspective

Wives, in the same way be submissive to your husbands so that, if any of them do not believe the word, they may be won over without words by the behavior of their wives, when they see the purity and reverence of your lives. Your beauty should not come from outward adornment, such as braided hair and the wearing of gold jewelry and fine clothes. Instead, it should be that of your inner self, the unfading beauty of a gentle and quiet spirit, which is of great worth in God's sight. For this is the way the holy women of the past who put their hope in God used to make themselves beautiful. They were submissive to their own husbands, like Sarah, who obeyed Abraham and called him her master. You are her daughters if you do what is right and do not give way to fear.

1 Peter 3:1-6

There is so much covered in this passage that it would be easy to miss the best part. Tucked right in the middle of this passage is "of great worth in God's sight."

Great Worth

Can you imagine something being valuable to God? He is the creator. Doesn't he have everything? We read in the Bible that he doesn't need anything (Acts 17:25); however, 1 Peter 3:4 says that there is something that is of great worth to him.

The Greek word translated "great worth" is *poluteles.*

> **Definition:** *Poluteles* (pol-oo-tel-ace) the very end or limit with reference to price; of the highest cost, very expensive, very precious.[1]

Poluteles means the *very* end or limit. In other words, this is at the top of God's list of what he considers most precious to him.

What do you think God values? Is a gentle and quiet spirit something that you would have listed as one of the things that is highly valued by God?

What do you value the most? I have a diamond engagement ring that I cherish. I treat it with great care because of its value and its sentimental significance. I have many other things I value and protect, but they are not at the top of my list. My family tops my list. I would give up my life for them. They are priceless to me.

Sometimes it's not clear what we mean by the word great. If you are single and I set you up on a blind date and told you that this guy is great, you might ask me some questions. "What's great about him?" Or, "How great is 'great'?"

We often use the word great in a casual way. We might say that it's a "great" day, but we are only casually comparing the last few days. However, God is not saying "great" casually. *Poluteles* means the very end or limit with reference to value. This Greek word is also used in Mark 14:3-5.

> *... a woman came with an alabaster jar of very expensive [poluteles] perfume, made of pure nard. She broke the jar and poured the perfume on his head...It could have been sold for more than a year's wages...*
> *Mark 14:3-5*

This passage gives us more insight into the word *poluteles.* This perfume was worth more than a year's salary. Personally, I've never spent more than half of what I make in one day for perfume. Most perfumes today cost between $25 and $100. The most expensive perfume that I've ever seen cost $400 an ounce. But even that perfume would not be close in comparison to a perfume that cost more than a year's salary.

If you had a bottle of perfume that cost more than what you make in a year (or could make), how would you take care of it compared to your other perfumes? And how would you describe it compared to your other perfumes? I probably would repeat the word "very" several times just so that it is clear how valuable it is – "very, very, very expensive perfume." When you compare this perfume that was poured on Jesus with any other perfume, it is by far the most valuable.

When God says *poluteles* in 1 Peter 3:4, he means GREAT worth or VERY precious. This tops his list. A gentle and quiet spirit is of incredible worth to him.

Worksheet 2 – Great Worth

1. What do you value the most?

2. According to 1 Peter 3:1-6, what does God value?

3. Do you feel highly valued by God?

4. Have you actively pursued the qualities of a gentle and quiet spirit?

5. How does feeling valued impact you?

6. Consider what you cherish the most. Throughout today consider God cherishing you in that way.

7. Write a prayer asking God to help you understand how much he values a gentle and quiet spirit.

Devote yourselves to prayer, being watchful and thankful.
Colossians 4:2

Gentle

The Greek word translated "gentle" or "meek" is *praus*. There are three scriptures in the New Testament with the word *praus* in the original text.

> *Instead, it should be that of your inner self, the unfading beauty of a gentle [praus] and quiet spirit, which is of great worth in God's sight.*
>
> 1 Peter 3:4

> *Say to the Daughter of Zion, "See, your king comes to you, gentle [praus] and riding on a donkey, on a colt, the foal of a donkey."*
>
> Matthew 21:5

> *Blessed are the meek [praus], for they will inherit the earth.*
>
> Matthew 5:5

Definition: *Praus* (prah-ooce') The exercises of it are first toward God. It is that temper of spirit in which we accept his dealings with us as good without disputing or resisting and is closely linked with the word humility. It is only the humble heart which is also *praus*, and which, as such, does not fight against God. *Praus* is the opposite of self-assertiveness and self-interest.

The meaning of *praus* is not readily expressed in English, for the terms gentleness and meekness, commonly used, suggest weakness, whereas *praus* does nothing of the kind. The common assumption is that when a man is meek or gentle, it is because he cannot help himself, but the Lord was *praus* because he had the infinite resources of God at his command.[2]

Praus means power under control, or power that is submitted or surrendered. It takes great inner strength to be *praus*. The English word gentleness refers more to actions, whereas *praus* refers more to a condition of mind and heart.[3] Our modern usage for "gentle" and "meek" is being mild or weak, lacking in spirit and courage. Having no inner strength and being easily imposed upon is how some people perceive a gentle and quiet spirit. Maybe that's the way Pilate viewed Jesus in Matthew 27:13-14, but Jesus was not replying *because* he had inner strength. Consider Jesus in the following verse. Imagine this taking place.

Say to the Daughter of Zion, "See, your king comes to you, gentle [praus] and riding on a donkey, on a colt, the foal of a donkey."

Matthew 21:5

Do you picture Jesus looking docile as he rode a donkey into Jerusalem? Read the definition of *praus* again and think about Jesus entering Jerusalem. When it says Jesus was *praus*, it's describing his attitude toward God. Jesus knew he was facing crucifixion, yet he was willing to go into Jerusalem. He was *praus*.

When Jesus was arrested, he said in Matthew 26:53, "Do you think I cannot call on my Father, and he will at once put at my disposal more than twelve legions of angels?" A legion is an army of up to 5,000 men.[4] So Jesus is saying that he could have immediately called more than 60,000 angels. One would have been enough! He had this infinite power that we cannot fathom. Consider this for a moment. Jesus was gentle (*praus*) because he had incredible power at his disposal and he chose not to use it. Instead he submitted himself to God and made himself available for God's plan for his life. He was gentle to God.

Was this how you described a "gentle" woman in the first worksheet? When I studied the Greek word *praus* and found that it described a strong woman instead of a weak one, it drastically changed how I read this verse. I found it more appealing.

Quiet

The Greek word for "quiet" is *hesuchios*.

> **Definition:** *Hesuchios* (hay-soo'-khee-os) tranquillity arising from within,[5] undisturbed and undisturbing, peaceable, and quiet.[6]

As a young child, I lived near a spring of water where my father would fill our water cans. Someone had put a concrete liner in the ground around the spring so that it was easy to draw the water out. I loved to go there. It was a peaceful place where water constantly bubbled up from within the earth and overflowed. It was puzzling to me how year after year the water kept coming. There was an invisible underground source that I could not understand as a child. I think of that spring every time I read this definition of "tranquillity arising from within." The quiet spirit also has an unseen source. It comes from a deep trust in God's love, protection and promises.

There are a lot of things we face every day that reveal whether or not we have this kind of spirit. Does "tranquillity arising from within" describe you or would the words "stressed-out" be a better fit? Stress, not tranquillity, describes many women today. Think back on what the last week has been like for you and your household. Were you undisturbed by the events you faced and undisturbing to others around you? Did you raise your voice or somehow lose control? Were you peaceful in the middle of all your busyness? Now, I assume you have been busy. We aren't talking about whether or not you have a life of leisure; we are talking about an inner quality.

Again, Jesus is the perfect example of *hesuchios*. Large crowds of people who were needy, hungry and sick often surrounded him (sounds like a family at times). Luke 8:42 says, "As Jesus was on his way, the crowds almost crushed him." It goes on to say that a woman touched him and that Jesus took the time to inquire about it. Unlike his disciples, who urged Jesus to send needy people away (Mark 6:36), Jesus was unruffled by the crowds. We also read about him sleeping in a boat during a storm. You can see his incredible peace and his trust in God as he deals with his disciples' fear (Matthew 8:23-26).

Jesus completely trusted God. Consider the following passage:

> *For I did not speak of my own accord, but the Father who sent me commanded me what to say and how to say it. I know that his command leads to eternal life. So whatever I say is just what the Father has told me to say.*
> *John 12:49-50*

He knew that God's commands would lead him to eternal life, in other words, get him back to heaven. He trusted God completely, including what to say and how to say it. What a remarkable level of trust!

There are many scriptures that give us direction on what to say and not say and how to say it and not say it. It's my goal to trust God completely, but occasionally my lack of tranquillity shows me that I am not. When

I'm in a stressful situation is when I'm most apt to say and do things that I later regret. At these times, I can usually find that I'm not trusting God about something. Consider the following scriptures:

> *May the God of hope fill you with all joy and peace as you trust in him, so that you may overflow with hope by the power of the Holy Spirit.*
>
> *Romans 15:13*

> *Trust in him at all times, O people; pour out your hearts to him, for God is our refuge.*
>
> *Psalms 62:8*

> *Do not let your hearts be troubled. Trust in God; trust also in me.*
>
> *John 14:1*

The quiet spirit is not a "fluff" quality. It comes from a deep trust in God's love, protection and promises.

Worksheet 3 – Gentle & Quiet

1. Have your definitions of gentle and quiet changed any from what you wrote in Worksheet 1? If so, how? Rewrite the definitions according to what you just learned.

2. Jesus described himself as gentle in the following verse. With the biblical definition of gentle in mind, how would this quality make him more approachable?

   Take my yoke upon you and learn from me, for I am gentle [praios – a form of praus] and humble in heart, and you will find rest for your souls.

   Matthew 11:29

3. Can you think of times in the life of Jesus when it would have been difficult for him not to use the power he had available?

4. Does "tranquillity flowing from within" describe you or are you stressed-out?

5. What causes you the most stress?

6. Is your marriage peaceful? (If you are single, are you peaceful as a single woman?)

7. Write a prayer asking God to help you grow in a gentle and quiet spirit.

...those who seek the Lord lack no good thing.
Psalm 34:10

Summary

1 Peter 3:1-6 describes an amazing woman. She is a woman with great inner strength, who has a close relationship with God. She trusts God to direct her, and she is overflowing with peace. She is both *praus* and *hesuchios*.

Was this a new perspective for you of "gentle," "quiet" and "great worth"? If it is, reading this once will probably not be enough. Romans 12:2 says, "Do not conform any longer to the pattern of this world, but be transformed by the renewing of your mind." Renewal is a process. That's why we need to read the Bible often.

Throughout this book, I will review the definitions of gentle and quiet. Without a clear picture of what we are aiming for, it's hard to make progress. These incredible qualities are available to each of us. Having God's perspective about how much he values them will motivate us when it seems difficult. One of my reference books described *praus* as an "inwrought grace of the soul."[7] Inwrought means worked or woven into a fabric, like the yarn of a beautiful tapestry or needlework. It's a process that takes time, but it's time well spent.

- Chapter 2 -

A New Heart

... if any of them do not believe the word, they may be won over without words by the behavior of their wives, when they see the purity and reverence of your lives.

1 Peter 3:1-2

According to this passage, a wife can win her husband over in a most peculiar way – without words! I have thought that "without words" must be the most difficult instruction in the Bible. I usually have something to say! I've tried winning my husband over with many words, and occasionally I succeeded; however, it often created a very tense situation. I have had a lot of arguments with God about the "without words" part. "God, what if Jim makes a mistake? What if he did not understand what I was saying? Shouldn't I say it again, because he doesn't seem to understand my point of view?" Occasionally I did try the "without words" approach, but it was with a bitter spirit, better known as the silent treatment.

Actually, "without words" is only powerful if it is combined with a pure and reverent life. According to this passage, you can win over your husband with purity and reverence. Purity and reverence need to be observable. It isn't about knowledge – it is your life. I have seen my husband reverse his course of action when I responded to him in a reverent way.

PURITY AND REVERENCE ARE KEYS TO THE GENTLE AND QUIET SPIRIT.

Purity and reverence are actually keys to the gentle and quiet spirit. It took me a long time to understand this. Remember that *praus* is more than a person's outward behavior – it is exercised first toward God. Consider the New American Standard Bible version of 1 Peter 3:3-4:

> *Your adornment must not be merely external—braiding the hair, and wearing gold jewelry, or putting on dresses; but let it be the hidden person of the heart, with the imperishable quality of a gentle and quiet spirit, which is precious in the sight of God.*
>
> *1 Peter 3:3-4 (NASB)*

The "hidden person of the heart" is the real you. In my early years of marriage, I tried to become gentle and quiet by putting on an act, but it was usually short-lived. I would do well for awhile when my days were smooth and there was no pressure, but often when something would happen that upset me, my reaction was not one of self-control. Once I got so angry that I threw a frozen roast across the kitchen in a fit of rage! A fit of rage is the opposite of surrendered and peaceful. After a fit of rage, I would feel so guilty and would promise myself that I would never do that again. The problem was that I did not know how to build the foundation on which to make this change. You must first work on the "hidden person of the heart." The gentle and quiet spirit is as much about being as doing. I needed to start with the foundation of purity and reverence to begin developing a gentle and quiet spirit. I needed a new heart.

I want to caution you not to jump to the "doing" part too early. You could read through this study quickly and not take the time to consider how you need to change. Deep character change takes time. Take the time to complete the worksheets and pray about these areas of your life. It is important to first understand the "being" part. As I said, I

18

have tried to put on the gentle and quiet spirit from the outside, instead of the inside – you know, the fake-it-till-you-make-it idea. However, changing from the inside out is much more effective. Jesus warned the Pharisees about cleaning the outside of the cup and leaving the inside dirty (Matthew 23:26). The Pharisees focused on their actions more than the heart behind their actions. So first soak up all you can about the heart that you need to have.

THE FIRST KEY - REVERENCE

There are three verses in the New Testament specifically directed to women or wives about being reverent.

1)   Reverence For God - 1 Peter 3:2

In 1 Peter 3:2, the Greek word translated "reverence" is *phobos*.

> *...when they see the purity and reverence [phobos] of your lives.*
>
> *1 Peter 3:2*

Definition: *Phobos* (fob'-os) fear, dread or terror, a reverential fear of God as a controlling motive of life in spiritual and moral matters. It is not a mere fear of his power and righteous retribution, but a wholesome dread of displeasing him. It is a fear that influences the disposition and attitude of one whose circumstances are guided by trust in God. Reverential fear of God will inspire a constant careful-ness in dealing with others in his fear.[8]

Fear, dread and terror do not make a pretty picture. Reading this defini-tion made me take note of my walk with God. It describes a woman who is very serious about her relationship with God, a woman who has an awe of God. She has a wholesome dread of displeasing God, but does not shrink from him in terror. So should I fear God or love him? Both! God has demonstrated an incredible love for us, and he holds our eternity in his hands.

Sometimes it's helpful to look at the opposite of something to gain a better understanding. An example of irreverence is the story of Uzzah in 2 Samuel 6:1-19 when David was moving the ark of the covenant. (If you don't remember the story, take a few minutes right now and read it.) The ark of the covenant was a chest of wood that was covered inside and out with gold (Exodus 25:10-16). It was considered very holy. David decided to move it, but instead of having the men of the Kohathite tribe carry it (Numbers 4:15), he put it on a new cart pulled by oxen. When the oxen stumbled, Uzzah reached out and took hold of the ark to keep it from falling. Uzzah died because of his "irreverent act."

I WOULDN'T TOUCH THAT IF I WERE YOU!

Uzzah is an example of irreverence. In the past I have thought, "Poor Uzzah, he was just trying to help! Why did he have to die?" After studying reverence for God, I began to understand. God had made it very clear how to move the ark. At every turn, God's instructions were ignored. Uzzah's disregard for God's word was irreverent.

Disregarding God's word about marriage would be irreverent. God has clearly set out that he wants a wife to follow her husband's lead. But today these scriptures are frequently disregarded. Don't be like Uzzah. Don't touch it! Don't touch the leadership of your marriage. Maybe you won't die on the spot, but a little of your blissful marriage will.

There have been numerous times in my marriage when I stepped into the leadership role because I was trying to help. At times I refused to submit to Jim's leadership because I thought I had a better idea. Staying out of the leader role can be challenging. This takes reverence for God, because your husband may make a mistake like David. What if he does make a mistake? Actually, the better question is: What will God think of you taking over? Will it honor God?

What if Uzzah had let the ark fall to the ground? I don't know the answer to that, but I do know it wasn't Uzzah's place to touch it. David was not obeying God, but it still wasn't Uzzah's place to touch the ark. David eventually got it right (1 Chronicles 15:1-2); however, Uzzah was not around to enjoy the celebration.

God has given us very specific instructions about how to be a godly wife so that we will receive the blessings of a great marriage. He wants to bless us, but we must trust him. If you are not completely surrendered to God in your life, you will find it difficult to grow in a gentle and quiet spirit. It's an issue of trust. There are some questions we have to resolve in our minds before we will totally trust God: Does God know what he is talking about? Does he mean what he says? Do the scriptures about women in the Bible apply today or are they just a cultural guide from thousands of years ago?

There are many stories in the Bible that show that God means what he says. Uzzah is one example. We also learn a lot about God's teachings by putting them into practice. Consider these scriptures:

> *If anyone chooses to do God's will, he will find out whether my teaching comes from God or whether I speak on my own.*
> *John 7:17*

> *But the man who looks intently into the perfect law that gives freedom, and continues to do this, not forgetting what he has heard, but doing it—he will be blessed in what he does.*
> *James 1:25*

Uzzah may have thought the instructions about the ark of the covenant were archaic. Perhaps he had never heard them, but he found out they still applied to him.

Both men and women have struggled in their roles from the very beginning. Eve's independence in the Garden of Eden caused her downfall, then she passed the blame (Genesis 3:1-13). Eve did not trust God in her heart, neither did she surrender to God in her actions.

Women through the ages have had the same struggles as you and I. We want to love and be loved, and we want security for our families. We want to feel important and valued. The women of Bible times had these same desires. The scriptures have the same power for us today, and God's promises still hold true. Consider these verses in light of your marriage:

Jesus Christ is the same yesterday and today and forever.
Hebrews 13:8

Jesus answered, "It is written: 'Man does not live on bread alone, but on every word that comes from the mouth of God.'"
Matthew 4:4

And we have the word of the prophets made more certain, and you will do well to pay attention to it, as to a light shining in a dark place, until the day dawns and the morning star rises in your hearts. Above all, you must understand that no prophecy of Scripture came about by the prophet's own interpretation. For prophecy never had its origin in the will of man, but men spoke from God as they were carried along by the Holy Spirit.
2 Peter 1:19-21

We will do well to pay attention to the scriptures on marriage. They still apply to us today, and they hold the answers to any problems we may face. God has great plans for your marriage. Trust him.

Blessed is he whose help is the God of Jacob, whose hope is in the LORD his God, the Maker of heaven and earth, the sea, and everything in them— the LORD, who remains faithful forever.
Psalm 146:5-6

As I look back over the 30 years of my marriage, I can say from personal experience that God does know what he is talking about. He has helped me build a close, intimate marriage. My fears spurred on by the women's lib movement were unfounded. I love my role and I am in love with my husband. It came about by doing it God's way, not mine. I had to grow in my reverence for God to gain the things he has promised. And even though it was difficult at times, the blessings have been well worth the effort.

Worksheet 4 – Reverence for God

1. Write the definition of reverence (*phobos*).

2. Consider the following verses that contain the word *phobos* in the original text. Do you revere God?

   > *Since we have these promises, dear friends, let us purify ourselves from everything that contaminates body and spirit, perfecting holiness out of reverence [phobos] for God.*
   >
   > *2 Corinthians 7:1*

   > *Since you call on a Father who judges each man's work impartially, live your lives as strangers here in reverent [phobos] fear.*
   >
   > *1 Peter 1:17*

3. Is your reverence for God's word obvious to your husband?

4. Do you trust the scriptures regarding marriage?

5. Write a prayer asking God to help you grow in your reverence for him.

23

Pray continually.

1 Thessalonians 5:17

2)   Respect For Your Husband – Ephesians 5:33

The second verse about reverence is Ephesians 5:33. The Greek word is *phobeo*. *Phobeo* can be translated "reverence" or "respect."

> *...and the wife must respect [phobeo] her husband.*
>
> *Ephesians 5:33*

Definition: *Phobeo* (fob-eh'-o) to be frightened, to be alarmed; to be in awe of, i.e., revere; be afraid, fear, reverence.[9]

In this verse *phobeo* was translated "respect." I was taken aback when I read the definition of *phobeo*. What does it mean to respect your husband? As a teenager, I sang Aretha Franklin's lyrics: "R-E-S-P-E-C-T find out what it means to me." I knew what respect meant to me, but it wasn't what God had in mind. I have felt respect (*phobeo*) like this toward God, but I do not ever remember having a fear of my husband. There have been times I have had disdain for my husband rather than awe. It has taken me quite awhile to understand the impact this had on our relationship and how hard it would have been for Jim to lead me or even influence my thinking.

I had learned how to show dutiful respect to my husband, but even that was difficult at times, because I knew his weaknesses like no one else. So I was very challenged when I read the meaning of *phobeo*. This definition is more about feelings than actions. I decided I needed to fast and pray, because I wanted to start seeing my husband's best and respond to him in a way that showed a deeper respect and awe from my heart.

So, practically what does it mean to respect your husband? When you deeply respect someone, you speak in a manner and tone that makes your respect for them obvious to anyone listening – especially your husband. That means no talking down to him, never being demeaning or demanding. You respect his ideas and choices. When you are "in awe" of someone, you take their input and you seek their advice and allow them to influence your life. It means you listen to their input, even though you know their weaknesses.

John Gray, who wrote *Men Are From Mars, Women Are From Venus*, questioned over 25,000 people who participated in his relationship seminars. He states the following:

> The most frequently expressed complaint men have about women is that women are always trying to change them. When a woman loves a man, she feels responsible to assist him in growing and tries to help him improve the way he does things. She forms a home-improvement committee, and he becomes her primary focus. No matter how much he resists her help, she persists – waiting for any opportunity to help him or tell him what to do. She thinks she's nurturing him, while he feels he's being controlled. Instead, he wants her acceptance.[10]

Are you trying to shape up your husband? Can you imagine how frustrating it would be for him to feel unaccepted by you? When you don't accept something about him and become the "home-improvement committee," it can lead to some unhappy times in your marriage. I have listened as many tearful wives described their unhappy marriages, and they blamed it on their husbands. There was something their husbands needed to change and they all struggled to respect their men. Many tried to show their husbands respect, but instead of becoming more respectful, they more often became bitter. They were trying to improve the wrong person. They were irreverent to their husbands, and then they wondered what happened to their happy marriages. As it did with Uzzah, irreverence has its price.

Almost every woman I closely know has a challenge to some degree in showing this kind of respect to her husband. This is a very high calling. Some very spiritual women, who have devoted their lives to God, struggle with this. Being religious certainly does not mean you will automatically respect your husband. It's possibly more challenging, because you can become self-righteous when your husband is not living up to your expectations.

Do you see yourself as "spiritual"? How influential are you with your husband? Does your husband feel your deep respect or has he become your home-improvement project? Is your marriage close and joyful?

Following is a verse where *phobeo* is translated "reverence":

> *...The time has come for judging the dead, and for rewarding your servants the prophets and your saints and those who reverence [phobeo] your name, both small and great...*
>
> *Revelation 11:18*

I show you this verse to help you see the seriousness of this Greek word. We are called to *phobeo* God, and the scriptures also say a wife "must" *phobeo* her husband. As Christians, we revere the name of the Lord, but do we also revere and respect our husbands like Ephesians 5:33 instructs?

You are showing reverence for God when you deeply respect your husband. There is a definite connection. God has given us an instruction, and if you are tempted to think it doesn't apply to you, remember Uzzah. It doesn't say respect your husband if you think he has earned it.

I have spoken with Christian sisters who are full of bitterness about their marriages. Some contemplate divorce, because their husbands won't change. Some feel stuck and live in a lonely relationship with their husbands. They struggle to respect their husbands, and they do not understand the connection between their lack of respect and their loneliness.

Early in my marriage when we had unresolved conflicts, I thought I had made a big mistake and married the wrong man. Eventually, I realized that the issue was not that I needed a different husband, but that I needed to be different. I have a wonderful husband, who is worthy of my respect. When I began to see how much more respect I needed to have for God and my husband, I began to see the problem was not what my husband was doing, but what I was doing. When I started doing my part, I was amazed at the changes in my marriage and my husband.

One of the most challenging examples of respect I've ever looked at in the Bible is where Sarah called Abraham her master.

> *...like Sarah, who obeyed Abraham and called him her master [kurios].*
>
> *1 Peter 3:6*

Definition: *Kurios* (koo'-ree-os) supreme in authority, God, Lord, master, sir.[11]

Why did Sarah call Abraham her master? Was this just a cultural thing? I don't think so. This verse tells us that there are two things Sarah did to make herself beautiful to God: 1) She obeyed Abraham, and 2) she called Abraham her master. Calling Abraham her master was something that came out of her heart, not just her mouth. Sarah had learned to value what God valued. I believe that is why God holds her up as an example for us to follow. Have you ever thought of your husband as "supreme in authority" in your life?

Sarah is a good example, but it is easy to dismiss someone who lived thousands of years ago in a wilderness and a different culture. Today, if you look around, there are few noteworthy examples of women who deeply respect their husbands. Consider the popular movies and TV characters. Disrespectful, sassy attitudes are thought to be funny, and put-downs are a major part of the dialogue. I recently saw an advertisement promoting a TV show that said, "behind every successful man is a woman who is kicking his butt." It may be funny on TV, but disrespect in your marriage will not be funny. Jim and I enjoy teasing each other and we laugh a lot. There are a lot of ways to laugh and have fun that are not disrespectful.

I recently spoke with a waitress who told me she had gotten married the previous week. She told me how she and her husband were always bantering words back and forth but that she always got the last word. She said she had challenged him to show her that he could come up with something else to say, but he couldn't. She had a lot to say and none of it was in anyway respectful of her new husband. I know she was trying to be funny, but it was sad to hear her speak this way. I invited her to an upcoming marriage retreat. She laughed and said she didn't need that yet!

On another day I watched a middle-aged couple buying groceries. When he asked her about buying some broccoli for their dinner that evening, she scowled at him and said with a huff that they had eaten broccoli the night before. He then suggested corn. She didn't even answer him but, instead, gave him a harsh look and walked away. I'm sure this kind of disrespect has taken a huge toll on her marriage.

We are surrounded by disrespect. Rarely have I known a woman who respects her husband as called for in the scriptures. Even in meetings of the church, I have seen women roll their eyes at their husbands, argue, interrupt, or answer for their husbands. I have heard Christian women make harsh or derogatory comments about men. One wife said in a meeting, "We know men only use half their brain." She was trying to be funny, but I don't think any of the men who heard her thought so. We have been so influenced by the world around us. We need to step back and examine our words and our level of respect for the men in our lives.

Our world desperately needs examples of women who have an incredible respect for their husbands and their leadership. Not only that, but your husband needs to be encouraged and built up. He has a high calling by God too. His role is just as challenging as your role, and he needs your support and respect. Of course, it will be difficult to have this kind of respect without a deep trust in God. That's why we first looked at our reverence for God.

Worksheet 5 – Respecting Your Husband

1. Write the definition of respect (*phobeo*).

2. Do you deeply respect your husband? Describe the ways you respect him.

3. When is it most difficult for you to show him respect?

4. How do you show disrespect?

5. Write a prayer asking God to help you respect your husband as instructed in Ephesians 5:33.

He replied, "This kind can come out only by prayer."

Mark 9:29

3)   Consecrated to God – Titus 2:3

The third verse in regard to women being reverent is Titus 2:3.

> *Likewise, teach the older women to be reverent [hieroprepes]
> in the way they live, not to be slanderers or addicted to much
> wine, but to teach what is good.*
>
> *Titus 2:3*

The Greek word translated "reverent" in this verse is *hieroprepes.*

> **Definition:** *Hieroprepes* (hee-er-op-rep-ace') suited to a sacred
> character, that which is befitting in persons, actions or things con-
> secrated to God.[12]

Being consecrated to God means that you are totally devoted to him.
Something that has been consecrated is set aside for that purpose only.
Like the holy articles that were part of the worship in the temple, they
were used only for that purpose.

This is a special calling for older women. He wants them to be set aside
for his holy purpose, part of which is the great calling to teach the
younger women to love their husbands and children.

When I became an empty-nester, I was surprised at how much extra
time I had. I considered many ways to use this time. I could study for a
new career, take up new hobbies, travel, etc., and I have enjoyed some
of these things. However, God says that this is a special time to grow
in reverence.

Even if you are not old, you may be the "older" woman in your ministry
group and the one whom the other women look up to for help. Your
respect for your husband needs to be respect suited to a deeply spiritual
woman. Your walk needs to be louder than your talk. Then you will be
a woman worthy of imitation.

Titus 2:3 says to "teach" reverence. It's not something we would know
without some help. I appreciate my Christian sisters who have taught
me how to be a better wife. In the church we are blessed to have women
who take the time to teach us and help us grow spiritually. I especially
appreciate the openness of the women who have helped me. They have

taught me to be open and honest and have given me friendship and guidance. I personally want to take it higher as I teach and train other women, and I want to continue to grow in my reverence for God and my respect for my husband.

• – •

Worksheet 6 – Set Aside for God's Purpose

1. If you are an "older woman," how could you be more devoted to God by the way you live and by what you teach?

The second key to this new heart we are striving for is purity. The Greek word translated "purity" is *hagnos*.

> *...when they see the purity [hagnos] and reverence of your lives.*
>
> *1 Peter 3:2*

Definition: *Hagnos* (hag-nos') innocent, modest, perfect – chaste, clean, pure.[13]

We are called to be modest, innocent and pure. This would include our clothing, entertainment, speech, etc. Philippians 4:8 tells us to think about things that are pure (*hagnos*). Titus 2:3-5 instructs the older women to teach the younger women to be pure (*hagnos*). Regardless of age, gender or marital status, every Christian is to live a pure life (2 Corinthians 6:17 - 7:1).

How do you perceive someone who is pure? Do you equate purity with naivety and vulnerability? Women today are bombarded with the idea that a worldly woman is a strong woman. I think a better word to describe her would be "hardened." Becoming like God is how you become strong. We become pure like him by turning away from sinfulness (1 John 3:2-3). He promises us a spirit of power, love and self-discipline (2 Timothy 1:7).

I have seen the impact of pure actions and pure motives in my own marriage. I have watched my husband change his direction and his tone when I responded righteously during a disagreement. I have "won" him over by purity and reverence. Occasionally, as I have tried to be righteous, it still didn't resolve the situation. But my respectful response did prevent us from getting further entangled in a disagreement.

I want to have a higher goal than just resolving a situation. I want to be pure and reverent so that I can please God. There is also something else I need to consider. I may be wrong about what I think needs to happen, even though I feel very strongly about it at that moment. Imagine being wrong about something and feeling so strongly about it that you become unrighteous on top of being wrong!

There were times when I was very disrespectful as I fought with my husband. I have slammed doors, thrown things and said some very impure words. I even felt justified in my actions. But I have learned that I am completely dishonoring God when I am being unrighteous or disrespectful. Even if you feel stuck between a rock and a hard place, purity is always the right way. God will honor it and it will impress your husband too. Honor God by your actions and reactions. Sometimes I feel it takes all the strength I can muster to choose to do what's right rather than follow my feelings, but when I do, I find God works through these times quickly and effectively.

Besides pure actions, we must have pure motives. This is where it gets tricky. Why am I doing what I am doing? Are my motives pure?

> *All a man's ways seem right to him, but the LORD weighs the heart.*
>
> *Proverbs 21:2*

God knows the motives of my heart. My motives can be so deep that they are difficult to discern. I can start off with pure motives, but then somewhere along the way, I find that I have strayed. And I end up with an ulterior motive. I am tempted to get something else from it – like revenge! It is difficult for me to stay with my motivation to please God when there is pain involved. When I feel mistreated by my husband, I can easily fall into an agenda of hurting him back. Sometimes that comes in the form of a silent treatment, sometimes harsh words. I constantly have to test my motives and remind myself why I'm doing what I'm doing.

Bitterness

I think the greatest challenge I've had in having pure motivation has been bitterness in my heart. At times I would let something pass, but later I overreacted to a little incident because of bitterness stored up in my heart.

Bitterness is an ugly sin and very dangerous to a relationship. Synonyms for bitterness are resentment, unpleasantness, sullenness, anger, animosity and hostility. It seems there is no limit to the amount of bitterness a heart can hold. Consider the following verse:

> *The godless in heart harbor resentment...*
>
> *Job 36:13*

We are without God – godless – when we are bitter. Bitterness is a shifty sin because it disguises itself. I can feel right and justified when I have this sin in my heart. This verse uses the word "harbor." A harbor is a place where something is concealed and protected. So even though it feels right to protect bitterness in your heart, it's dangerous. You are actually far from God when you are bitter.

If you've been building up bitterness for years, it may take awhile to get through the layers. If you are open to input and seek it, I'm sure God will help you overcome it. Knowing it's not right to have it in your heart and actually digging it out are two different things. We must get rid of it (Ephesians 4:31).

After studying reverence and purity for many days, I didn't feel like I was changing, so I decided to fast from food for one day. At the end of that day, I still felt frustrated. I had a lot of dialogue going on in my head about why my husband was as much at fault as I was. I was struggling with bitterness. I prayed a great deal that day and asked God to help me become more reverent. I decided to fast another day the following week.

I don't completely understand the significance of fasting, but I do know it is a time to humble myself before God. After the second day of fasting, I began to catch myself before I would be disrespectful. Sometimes it was just in my heart and sometimes it was in my actions, but it was exciting to see progress. I have fasted other days in regard to this too.

After a couple of months of making progress, I prayed one morning asking God to help me see anything impure in my attitudes toward my husband. Before I ate my pancakes that morning, I had three different critical thoughts toward Jim that God revealed to me. I was convicted and encouraged at the same time. Convicted that I still had stuff coming out of my heart, yet encouraged that God had answered my prayer so quickly. It encourages me that God hears my prayers and answers me so clearly, and it also gives me comfort. I want to have a pure heart, and God wants to help me. Jim might never have known what was in my heart, but he would have felt its effects. Before I studied reverence, I probably wouldn't have been convicted about my disrespectful attitudes, because they were too often a part of my daily thoughts.

It's out of reverence for God that I will even begin the hard work of growing in my purity. Growing in purity means sinning less and that can be challenging, especially in marriage, because marriage is a twenty-four-hours-a-day, seven-days-a-week relationship. Your level of purity in your marriage says a great deal about your reverence for God and your respect for your husband. If you are unloving to your husband in your heart, you are not revering God. Remember that the definition of reverence is a wholesome dread of displeasing God and a reverential fear of God that will inspire a constant carefulness in dealing with others in his fear. This means how I feel and act toward my husband has a lot to say about my reverence for God. Consider the following verse in regard to your husband:

> *If anyone says, "I love God," yet hates his brother, he is a liar. For anyone who does not love his brother, whom he has seen, cannot love God, whom he has not seen.*
>
> *1 John 4:20*

Purity brings peace to me. I've had to battle my sinfulness to get here, but it was well worth the fight. I was beginning to fight the right person – me.

Worksheet 7 – Purity

1. What are the challenges you face to be pure in your actions toward your husband?

2. Do you struggle with these obstacles to purity?

   Bitterness: Job 36:13; Acts 8:23; Ephesians 4:31-32
   Anger: James 1:19-20; Matthew 5:22
   Impure thoughts: Proverbs 15:26; Titus 1:15-16
   Being unmerciful: Micah 6:8; Matthew 18:35
   Dutiful instead of a heart response: Isaiah 29:13; 1 Peter 1:22
   Arrogance: 1 Samuel 2:3; Proverbs 8:13
   Ungodly speech: Proverbs 10:19; Psalm 64:3; Colossians 3:8

3. Are you more apt to show respect in a dutiful way or is it from your heart?

4. Do you demonstrate more respect for your husband in public than in private

5. Do you feel justified when you respond to your husband in an unrighteous way?

6. Read Psalm 139 and write a prayer asking God to help you grow in your purity.

Watch and pray so that you will not fall into temptation.

Matthew 26:41

- Chapter 3 -

Fear of Submission

...like Sarah, who obeyed Abraham and called him her master.
You are her daughters if you do what is right and do not give
way to fear.

1 Peter 3:6

Isn't it interesting that 1 Peter 3:1-6 ends by encouraging us not to give in to fear? God is making sure everything is covered, because there are many fears in regard to submission. It's important to remember that submissiveness is not just for wives. Every Christian's life should be characterized by submission. When we look in the Bible, we find it's required of everyone. First we are to submit to God (Hebrews 12:9, James 4:7), then we are also called to submit to our governing authorities (Romans 13:1, 1 Peter 2:13), to church leaders (Hebrews 13:17), to those who work hard among us (1 Corinthians 16:16), and to one another (Ephesians 5:21). Submissiveness is listed as one of the qualities of the wisdom that comes from heaven (James 3:17). Again, Jesus is our example:

> *During the days of Jesus' life on earth, he offered up prayers*
> *and petitions with loud cries and tears to the one who could*
> *save him from death, and he was heard because of his rever-*
> *ent submission.*
>
> *Hebrews 5:7*

There are many scriptures that teach us the importance of a surrendered Christian life; however, there are several verses that specifically address wives:

> *Wives, in the same way be submissive to your husbands...*
> *1 Peter 3:1*

> *Wives, submit to your husbands as to the Lord.*
> *Ephesians 5:22*

> *Now as the church submits to Christ, so also wives should submit to their husbands in everything.*
> *Ephesians 5:24*

> *Wives, submit to your husbands, as is fitting in the Lord.*
> *Colossians 3:18*

Submission is not a popular topic today. It is very misunderstood by the modern woman, and her ideas are in opposition to what we read in the Bible. Many women today feel strongly that they need to stand up and fight for their rights. Now, I don't want to take away anyone's rights – that is not what this study is about. We could have our rights taken away and still not be submissive!

We can have many fears when it comes to letting our husbands lead us. Being a Christian does not exempt us from fears, but living like Jesus can help us overcome them.

What are some of our fears in this regard? Three that I want to address are: 1) fear of abasement, 2) fear of neglect, and 3) fear of abuse. It's important to challenge how you think about these to see if they have any impact on your relationship with your husband. Let's look at what the scriptures say in regard to these fears.

1)   The Fear of Abasement

Are you saying that as the leader, a husband is more intelligent, important or spiritual than I am? Will I look stupid if I submit? Will I have to live my life through him? Will I lose my self-respect? The fear of abasement is the fear that you will lose dignity or prestige or be humiliated.

The Greek word that is translated "submit" is *hupotasso*.

Definition: *Hupotasso* (hoop-ot-as'-so) to obey, submit self unto.[14]

The word *hupotasso* means to put oneself under the leadership of another. It's a voluntary act. If you humble yourself in a situation, that is your choice. Consider Jesus' example:

> *The reason my Father loves me is that I lay down my life—only to take it up again. No one takes it from me, but I lay it down of my own accord. I have authority to lay it down and authority to take it up again. This command I received from my Father.*
> John 10:17-18

What are our obstacles in following Jesus' example? One is that we are influenced in many ways about how we think of our role as a wife. Reading about women's history or watching a documentary about women in foreign countries today can stir us up and make us question the role of a wife. It seems everywhere I turn someone is defining a wife's role in a negative way. The following is an excerpt from *A Marriage Made in Heaven or Too Tired for an Affair* by Erma Bombeck:

> The priest was Polish and between his accent and the Latin of the Mass, I strained to interpret his words. Then loud and clear I heard him admonish, "You, Bill, are to be the head of the house and you, Erma, are to be the heart."
>
> In his dreams. What did he think he was dealing with here…a child who chose a nickel over a dime because it was bigger? I had seen the "heart detail" and I didn't struggle through four years of conjugating verbs to get choked up over my husband's high bowling scores. Maybe I could talk Bill into being the heart…or at least trade off once in a while.
>
> *"I now pronounce you man and wife."*
>
> With the possible exception of "We have lift-off" and "This country is at war," there are few phrases as sobering.[15]

I enjoy reading Erma's books – she is very funny. But this is an example of someone influencing us about our role as a wife. When we read something like Erma's book, it is easy to get stirred up in a bad way. I want to say, "Yeah, I'm with you, Erma!" If getting choked up over my husband's high bowling score is my role, I don't want that either. I have more to offer than that.

Consider the following excerpt from an article titled "A Good Wife's Guide" from *Housekeeping Monthly*, May 13, 1955:

> Listen to him. You may have a dozen important things to tell him, but the moment of his arrival is not the time. Let him talk first – remember his topics of conversation are more important than yours.

There wasn't a byline showing who wrote this. It's not all bad, but the general tone of the entire article was demeaning saying that your husband is important and you are not.

My purpose for including these quotations is that we are influenced in many ways by other peoples' perceptions about a wife's role. Who has shaped how you think a marriage should be? Was it Hollywood, your parents or God? Perhaps it has been a combination of these. Was it by watching a marriage that brought you a lot of pain as a child?

One response I had to the negative ideas about a submissive wife was to try to define my own role so I could protect myself. However, as I have already said, my model didn't work very well. I have since learned that God has an incredible plan for the roles of husband and wife.

> *The LORD God said, "It is not good for the man to be alone. I will make a helper [ezer] suitable for him."*
>
> *Genesis 2:18*

The Hebrew word translated "helper" is *ezer*.

Definition: *Ezer* (ay'-zer) aid; help.[16]

The following two quotes have helped me better understand this Hebrew word:

> This is a notoriously difficult word to translate. It means something far more powerful than just "helper"; it means "lifesaver." The phrase is only used elsewhere of God, when you need him to come through for you desperately. Eve is a life giver; she is Adam's ally.[17]

To most people a "helper" is a subordinate, an assistant who has no authority. They just tag along, waiting for someone important to tell them what to do. If the Maker of heaven and earth is a helper, I think it's clear that there is no shame in being a helper.[18]

The following verses are examples of the word *ezer* being used to describe God as a helper:

> *There is no one like the God of Jeshurun, who rides on the heavens to help [ezer] you...*
>
> Deuteronomy 33:26

> *My help [ezer] comes from the LORD, the Maker of heaven and earth.*
>
> Psalm 121:2

God is our helper because he is strong, capable and kind. He has something to offer us and we need his help. We have much to offer our husbands, and they need our help too. God said so!

This biblical definition of what it means to be a helper is quite a contrast both to Erma's book and "The Good Wife's Guide." But then God's thoughts are often not our thoughts.

> *"For my thoughts are not your thoughts, neither are your ways my ways," declares the LORD. "As the heavens are higher than the earth, so are my ways higher than your ways and my thoughts than your thoughts."*
>
> Isaiah 55:8-9

Another way to overcome the fear of abasement is to follow Jesus' example of humility. Consider the following passage:

> *Your attitude should be the same as that of Christ Jesus: Who, being in very nature God, did not consider equality with God something to be grasped, but made himself nothing, taking the very nature of a servant, being made in human likeness. And being found in appearance as a man, he humbled himself and became obedient to death— even death on a cross! Therefore God exalted him to the highest place and gave him the name that is above every name.*
>
> Philippians 2:5-9

This is the attitude we should have as Christians in every aspect of our lives, which would also include our role in marriage. This attitude of humility is for both a husband and wife. Our husbands also have special instruction about how to lead:

> *Also a dispute arose among them as to which of them was considered to be greatest. Jesus said to them, "The kings of the Gentiles lord it over them; and those who exercise authority over them call themselves Benefactors. But you are not to be like that. Instead, the greatest among you should be like the youngest, and the one who rules like the one who serves. For who is greater, the one who is at the table or the one who serves? Is it not the one who is at the table? But I am among you as one who serves.*
>
> *Luke 22:24-27*

> *Not so with you. Instead, whoever wants to become great among you must be your servant, and whoever wants to be first must be your slave—just as the Son of Man did not come to be served, but to serve, and to give his life as a ransom for many.*
>
> *Matthew 20:26-28*

> *Husbands, love your wives, just as Christ loved the church and gave himself up for her.*
>
> *Ephesians 5:25*

This sounds good to me! I'm asked to submit myself to my husband, who has been asked to lead me by giving himself up for me, serving me and loving me. (That's the nutshell version.) Does that describe your marriage? Hopefully, but if it doesn't, God has a plan to help you bring about a change.

Remember that gentle (*praus*) means "a temper of spirit in which we accept God's dealings with us as good without disputing or resisting and is closely linked with the word humility. It is only the humble heart which is also meek or gentle and which, as such, does not fight against God." A humble person is in a powerful position. God says he is on the side of the humble person (James 4:6). Consider the following scriptures on humility:

He guides the humble in what is right and teaches them his way.

Psalm 25:9

Humble yourselves before the Lord, and he will lift you up.
James 4:10

Humility and the fear of the LORD bring wealth and honor and life.

Proverbs 22:4

We have to let God, not popular opinion, define our roles. If you look at what popular opinion has brought the people who follow these modern ideas, it's not very attractive – neither in quality nor in longevity of their relationships. God has set us up for a great marriage if we will trust him to direct us in our roles. He does not want to humiliate us, but he does want us to be humble. Being submitted has nothing to do with your importance or intelligence. Actually, it shows a great inner strength *(praus)* and trust in God. Jesus was certainly intelligent, important and spiritual, but he still let God direct his life. He also looked to God for his strength and confidence. God was able to do some incredibly powerful things through Jesus' life, because Jesus submitted himself to God. God's response to Jesus was to exalt him to the "highest place." (Philippians 2:9)

My husband also wants to build me up, encourage me and protect me when I am humble and seek his leadership. He honors me in many ways. I had a lot of fears about submission from the start of my marriage, and these fears were unfounded. We have heard so much about a woman's rights in our culture that being humble in our role as a wife has now become offensive. As I have learned to be humble and trust God in my role as a wife, I have been blessed in many, many ways. One of those blessings is an inner peace or tranquillity *(hesuchios)* that I did not have before I began trusting these scriptures. When I was arrogant and unyielding, there was no peace – in my life or his!

Worksheet 8 – Fear of Abasement

1. Do you think a wife's role is inferior to a husband's role?

2. Who or what has had the most *negative* influence on how you view your role? Who or what has had the greatest *positive* influence on how you view your role?

3. Consider the following verses. Do you think Jesus would have been able to accomplish the work God had given him if he had not been completely submitted to God's leadership?

    > But the world must learn that I love the Father and that I do exactly what my Father has commanded me.
    >
    > *John 14:31*

    > For I did not speak of my own accord, but the Father who sent me commanded me what to say and how to say it. I know that his command leads to eternal life. So whatever I say is just what the Father has told me to say.
    >
    > *John 12:49-50*

4. Are you afraid of being humble? What is your greatest challenge in being humble with your husband?

5. Write a prayer asking God to help you grow in your humility.

But I cry to you for help, O LORD; in the morning my prayer comes before you. — Psalm 88:13

48

2)   The Fear of Neglect

If I submit to his leadership, can I trust him to take care of my needs? What if he ignores me?

Do you feel neglected by your husband? In response to this fear, the goal of many women is to be strong, confident and accomplished so they won't be dependent upon a man. It would be great to be strong, confident and accomplished, but independence stands against the idea of "becoming one" in the first place. It doesn't work. Independence within a marriage will break down intimacy.

If you find neglect in your marriage, how do you deal with it? Did you know that there is a deep-rooted desire in a man to please his wife?

> *But a married man is concerned about the affairs of this world—how he can please his wife...*
> *1 Corinthians 7:33*

Do you believe your husband is concerned with how to please you? It says so in the Bible! What kind of man did you marry? Was he neglectful of you when you dated? I hope not. Most of us would not marry someone who was selfish or neglectful. I married a man who loved to do things for me, take me places and show me his love.

So, if you feel neglected, how can you tap into this desire of your husband? I want you to consider that, perhaps, there is something you can do to draw closer to your husband. I have noticed a common response in many wives. Often after an argument, the wife moves away emotionally from her husband. What I mean is, she has hurt feelings and she is waiting for an apology. I have also responded the same way. There were times when Jim and I would have an argument in the morning. By the end of the day, Jim would act like nothing had happened, but I would still be brooding over it. I was still hurt and I felt he *owed* me an apology. I could feel hurt for days. And if something else happened during those next few days, I would become even more hurt.

I have seen this scenario with many wives. Often the pattern is repeated again and again. What I'm trying to describe is an emotional separation, not a physical one. It goes like this. After a disagreement, the wife turns her back to her husband emotionally. He doesn't apologize and she takes a step away from him emotionally. He still doesn't respond and she takes another step. After years of this, a wife may wonder what happened, because she feels lonely and neglected. This distancing isn't the only reason a wife may feel neglected, but it is an area that might affect your closeness to your husband.

For the most part, if you are moving away from him in an emotional way, he is not going to follow you. It doesn't work that way. If you are headed off in an opposite direction from him because you are hurt, chances are he won't even understand what's happening. This process can become a downward spiral in a relationship.

Our sensitivity serves us well in many ways, but our sensitivity can hinder us too. If you feel lonely, are you waiting for something from your husband? I encourage wives to move back toward their husbands. It takes vulnerability, but vulnerability will build great intimacy. Ditch the hurt feelings and snuggle up to your man. He doesn't even remember why you are so upset!

Another solution to the problem of loneliness is looking at the level of respect you have for your husband. As a young wife, I set up a dynamic in my marriage that did a lot of damage to my relationship with my husband when I was disrespectful, controlling or demanding. The world says this transition happens because "the honeymoon is over." I believe it happens because a wife is out of her role. After 30 years of marriage, when I'm in my role as defined in the Bible, I've had many great "honeymoon" days.

The level of respect you give your husband can have a huge impact in drawing you closer together. You may be thinking that your husband doesn't listen to a thing you say, but your words can create a tension in your relationship and put a distance between you that can cause you to feel neglected and lonely.

> *Better to live in a desert than with a quarrelsome and ill-tempered wife.*
>
> *Proverbs 21:19*

Do your words draw your husband to you or drive him away? If you feel neglected and lonely, you should evaluate your words and consider their impact.

> *He who loves a pure heart and whose speech is gracious will have the king for his friend.*
>
> *Proverbs 22:11*

Do you want a better friendship with your husband? This verse says the key to that is a pure heart and gracious speech. We have already studied purity and the power of a pure-hearted response, but what does gracious speech mean?

The word "grace" simply means "favor." Gracious speech means showing favor through your speech. Consider all the ways God shows us his grace or his favor. His favor results in kindness, compassion, forgiveness, love, patience, faithfulness, etc. Consider how you speak to your husband. Do your words show him favor? When you speak about your husband, does it sound like you favor him?

A great biblical example of a woman who was gracious is Esther. She was taken to the king's palace as a young woman. As a young Jewish girl, I doubt it was her dream to be the new bride of a pagan king who had just dethroned his queen.

Her parents had died when she was young, and Mordecai, her cousin, had adopted her and brought her up in his home (Esther 2:7-15). Mordecai was distraught about her being taken away. He paced back and forth every day near the harem to find out what was happening to her (Esther 2:11). We are told that Esther obeyed instructions from Mordecai, and she took advice from those around her.

Esther became the new queen, but something happened that shook up her world. Her husband, the king, made a "bad" decision and gave permission to an evil man to kill the Jewish people – which included Esther. So Esther needed to get her husband to rethink this decision. She needed to win him over. Can you relate? Well, maybe we are not on the same level as Esther, but I think the principle is the same. She sought God's help in her fear, and she asked others to seek God's help for her. She fasted and prayed and went to the king.

I believe the king was very smitten by her, because twice he offered her half of his kingdom (Esther 5:3, 6). To get a perspective of how much he had, it says in Esther 1:4 that for a full 180 days he displayed the *vast* wealth of his kingdom and the splendor and glory of his majesty. But when the king offered her half of his kingdom, she only requested his presence at dinner. Wow! I'm impressed.

In the past I have thought that Esther chickened-out when he gave her this opportunity to ask him for anything and she only requested his presence at dinner. Instead, I believe she showed a lot of restraint and graciousness (kindness, courtesy and compassion). In other words, she did him a favor (showed him grace). I don't know who would have been there at the time she first approached him in the king's hall (Esther 5:1), but there were officials around him. There would have been guards there to protect him and remove her if he had chosen to do so. How embarrassing it would have been if she had told him of the situation at that time. He had just signed the death warrant of his queen. Oops, that's embarrassing! Esther was waiting for the right time to make her request, so she invited him to dinner.

At dinner that night, she decided the time was not yet right, so she asked him to come to dinner again the next night. Esther had just spent three days fasting. I believe the Spirit delayed her, because there were some things God still needed to put into place. The following night at dinner, she made her request, and she did it in a very gracious way. She not only became a great example to the Persian and Median women of how to respect their husbands (Esther 1:18-20), but to us as well. Esther is a great example of a godly woman married to an unbeliever. She was gracious and spiritual, and she influenced her husband.

Consider the impact on Esther's relationship with her husband if she had made her request with an edge or attitude. Consider how this scene would play out on a television sitcom. It might go something like this: "Have you lost your mind?!" Or what if Esther had gone to the king with hurt feelings and had not restrained her emotions? What if she had said, "How could you do this to me?!" He would have felt attacked. Of course, this was not a typical Christian marriage. He was a powerful pagan king. She could have done a lot of damage to her relationship with the king if she had not been gracious. Her respect and her graciousness brought them closer. I believe Esther won over her husband in a greater way than just having her request granted.

Her graciousness showed respect for the king. (Remember that respect or *phobeo* means "to be frightened, to be alarmed; to be in awe of, i.e., revere; be afraid, fear, reverence.") Your husband may not have the same powerful position as the king did, but you can still treat him with the respect fit for a king, and your graciousness will have the same kind of influence.

There are many aspects of gracious speech. I favor my husband by my words when they are compassionate, kind, respectful, considerate, affirming, encouraging, truthful and grateful. Gracious speech is not easily summarized.

GRACIOUS SPEECH REVEALS A DEEP RESPECT FOR YOUR HUSBAND.

It will be hard to grow in gracious speech unless you work on your heart. Consider this verse:

> *The good man brings good things out of the good stored up in his heart, and the evil man brings evil things out of the evil stored up in his heart. For out of the overflow of his heart his mouth speaks.*
>
> *Luke 6:45*

If you are lonely, I want to encourage you to look at 1) whether you are emotionally vulnerable with your husband and 2) whether you speak in a gracious way to him. Putting these two things into practice in a marriage can help build a lot of closeness and overcome neglect.

Worksheet 9 – The Fear of Neglect

1. Do you feel neglected or lonely in your marriage? If so, is this a new pattern in your marriage or was your marriage like this from the beginning?

2. Do you tend to hide out emotionally after a disagreement with your husband?

3. Are you willing to be vulnerable with your husband? What impact does this have on your relationship?

4. Would you characterize your communication with your husband as gracious (kind, courteous, grateful and compassionate)?

5. Write a prayer asking God to help you focus on your words and attitudes toward your husband so you can see any area in which you could be more respectful and gracious toward him.

Therefore let everyone who is godly pray to you while you may be found.

Psalm 32:6

3)   The Fear of Abuse

Abuse is a very serious matter. Fear of abuse covers a wide range of issues, from being taken advantage of to being physically hurt. If I submit to him, will he use me? Will I be a rug to him? What if he hurts me?

I have known some women who have never experienced any abuse, yet they still have this fear, and it affects their marriages. Because they generally don't trust men, they won't follow their husbands' lead. When I got married, I would not use the word "obey" in my marriage vows. I wanted some kind of safeguard as I entered into this relationship.

My fears spurred on by the women's lib movement created a bad dynamic in my marriage, and it was unfair to my husband. He had done nothing but show me his love before we got married. I was essentially saying that I didn't trust my husband or God's plan for my husband to be the leader in our marriage.

Abuse

Abuse is a reality in some marriages. I want to say upfront that I am not an authority on abuse. I have been very close to women who were in abusive relationships and have felt the burden of their pain, but that does not make me an expert on the subject. Books have been written on abuse, but this is not one of them. The purpose of this book is to help you grow in a gentle and quiet spirit. Those qualities may not impact an abusive husband. Grow in the ways you can, but be open and seek help if you are in an abusive relationship.

From my limited experience, I know that sometimes it is hard for an abused wife to be open and seek help. They are embarrassed about the abuse, and it brings out so many emotions. Some women feel there is no other option for them, so they stay in the abuse year after year. If you have needs in this area, please seek help.

Alcoholism and drug addiction are forms of abuse. If your husband has a drug or alcohol problem or addictions of any kind, it is very important for you to be open and seek help. Help is available for women who face this challenge. I would encourage you to seek the help of someone who has experience helping couples deal with chemical dependency or other addictions. You may be codependent. That can make his recovery difficult. Women who live with these challenges have a hard time knowing where and when to submit to their husbands. Supporting someone's addiction is not what submission is about.

Verbal Fights

You may never deal with physical abuse, but there is another whole area of abuse – verbal fights. In a disagreement, our words can be very abusive and hurtful. You may have lived in an environment where you have verbally abused each other for years. Occasionally it is a lopsided situation, but in most of the situations where my husband and I have helped married couples, it was a problem for both the husband and the wife.

In the early years of my marriage, I had a hot temper and I felt free to verbally fight with my husband. I have raised my voice and said rude and unkind remarks. As I look back on it, I cannot understand why I felt justified to speak so terribly. Today I have a deep conviction that verbal battles with my husband are ungodly. Verbal fights are such a waste of precious time and a tool of Satan to attack a marriage.

I'm not saying there aren't times to disagree, but your tone can make a big difference.

> *A gentle answer turns away wrath, but a harsh word stirs up anger.*
>
> *Proverbs 15:1*

If I have a different opinion from Jim, I will tell him what I think, but it is my goal to always do so in a respectful way. In the past when we have fought over issues and spent hours or days rehashing things, it has deeply hurt us both. The earlier things I wrote on purity and reverence have helped bring about the convictions that I needed to stop *my* wickedness and turn over the issues I could not control to God.

It is always sobering to do a study on godly speech. We all need to be careful with our speech.

If anyone considers himself religious and yet does not keep a tight rein on his tongue, he deceives himself and his religion is worthless.

James 1:26

But I tell you that men will have to give account on the day of judgment for every careless word they have spoken. For by your words you will be acquitted, and by your words you will be condemned.

Matthew 12:36-37

Praise God for his mercy and forgiveness! I've certainly needed much forgiveness from God because of my careless and angry words. I want to encourage you to consider ways to grow in godly speech. There are many blessings that come from repentance in this area. Consider these verses:

The tongue has the power of life and death, and those who love it will eat its fruit.

Proverbs 18:21

Do not repay evil with evil or insult with insult, but with blessing, because to this you were called so that you may inherit a blessing. For, "Whoever would love life and see good days must keep his tongue from evil and his lips from deceitful speech."

1 Peter 3:9-10

Pleasant words are a honeycomb, sweet to the soul and healing to the bones.

Proverbs 16:24

He who guards his mouth and his tongue keeps himself from calamity.

Proverbs 21:23

Turning around an emotionally charged atmosphere in a home can be challenging. Do you know how to calm the atmosphere with your husband? We often know how to push their buttons, but we need to learn how to turn around a moment that is headed off in the wrong direction. Let me share a few things that I've found to be effective.

If I feel hurt by a comment, a response I sometimes use is, "Ouch." I have found this very effective in helping me uncharge the atmosphere. My husband has responded quickly with an apology to this. It's a soft response, but it communicates a lot. Another way I uncharge the atmosphere with my husband is to affirm the obvious. If my husband expresses that he feels disrespected by me, I reaffirm my respect. If he is feeling unloved, I reaffirm my love. I get specific about it too. I may need to own up to something I said or did that discouraged him, but I can still reaffirm my love and respect for him. It helps uncharge the situation, and it's then easier to work through our problem. Another thing I've found helpful to uncharge a tense day when things are not going well for him is to give him a hug and tell him how much I love him. (I'll share more about this later.) I may not be able to solve his problem, but I can give him my love and support. There is an obvious improvement in the atmosphere when I do these things. These responses -- saying ouch, reaffirming the obvious and encouaging him when things aren't going well -- are not my natural responses. I've had to learn how to do this. (I will also share more about his later.)

I believe communication is one of the most challenging aspects of marriage. A soft and pure-hearted response can be very effective in working through differences. You can become a powerful, healing force in your marriage by the words you speak.

(The following worksheet covers more aspects of verbal fights. Be sure that you answer the questions and consider how these scriptures apply to you.)

Worksheet 10 – The Fear of Abuse

Abuse:

1. Are you in an abusive relationship? If so, write a prayer asking God to help you open up and get help.

Verbal Fights:

2. Do you have verbal fights with your husband?

3. Do you see any area in which you should be more self-controlled in your speech?

4. Are you easily angered in your relationship with your husband? Consider the following verses:

   Mockers stir up a city, but wise men turn away anger.
   Proverbs 29:8

   A fool gives full vent to his anger, but a wise man keeps himself under control.
   Proverbs 29:11

5. Strife can make our lives miserable in the midst of great blessings. Is your home known for its peace or its strife? Consider the following verse:

   Better a dry crust with peace and quiet than a house full of feasting, with strife.
   Proverbs 17:1

6. Are you quick to quarrel?

   It is to a man's honor to avoid strife, but every fool is quick to quarrel.
   Proverbs 20:3

7. Have you had conversations that could be characterized as wicked madness?

> *Words from a wise man's mouth are gracious, but a fool is consumed by his own lips. At the beginning his words are folly; at the end they are wicked madness—*
>
> *Ecclesiastes 10:12-13*

8. Have you recently vented your anger toward your husband? If so, how did it impact your relationship?

9. Read Psalm 141:3. Write a prayer asking God for wise words to bring about a more peaceful relationship with your husband.

Is any one of you in trouble? He should pray.
James 5:13

- Chapter 4 -

Sarah's Daughters

...like Sarah, who obeyed Abraham and called him her master. You are her daughters if you do what is right and do not give way to fear.

1 Peter 3:6

In the past I thought 1 Peter 3:1-6 exclusively applied to women married to unbelievers, so I did not benefit from the wisdom of this passage. In actuality, this scripture is written to every Christian wife. The passage begins very simply, "Wives, in the same way be submissive to your husbands." Then the following verses provide wisdom on how to successfully put submission into practice, how to think about submission, and how to approach submission if you are facing a less than ideal situation.

I picture a group of wives hearing this message about wives submitting to their husbands and responding, "I can accept that I should submit to my husband if he is a faithful, godly man, but what if he is ungodly? I don't have to submit to him, do I?" Peter was clearing up any confusion they might have. He then encouraged the wives who would face this challenge by telling them how to be very influential with their unbelieving husbands.

In verse 1 the Greek word that is translated "do not believe the word" is *apeitheo*.

Definition: *Apeitheo* (ap-i-theh'-o) disobedient, obey not, unbelieving.[19]

Peter tells us to be submissive to our husbands "so that, if" they are disobedient to God, we can influence them by our example of a pure and reverent life. In verse 6, Sarah is held up as an example for us. She was married to Abraham. He was a man of faith, but even Abraham had times when he struggled to trust God. So whether you are married to someone who is faithful like Abraham or not, you can learn some great lessons from the holy women of the past.

There are two "ifs" in becoming a daughter of Sarah. You are her daughter: 1) if you do what is right and 2) if you do not give way to fear. Our fears can take a big toll on our marriages. The fears we have can cause many "fights" with our husbands. You may call it an argument, a bump, a disagreement or something else, but I'm speaking of a conflict between a husband and wife that creates tension and steals their joy.

One way we might fight is by sending a loud and clear message, "I will get my way or else!" As Christians, we know that this is not right. Another more creative way, that on the outside seems to be more acceptable, is to take control of the situation. What does control look like? Nagging, arguing, bossiness, ultimatums, anger, fits of rage, forcefulness, the silent treatment, etc. The purpose of an ultimatum is to get your way. "If you don't do what I want, I'll...!" Maybe it will take the form of a fit of rage or a cold shoulder. Though at opposite extremes, they are both controlling. We do these things to try to force our husbands to modify their behavior.

You may be thinking, "So, what's your point?" My point is that if you live this way in your marriage, you are out of your role as a wife. I have found that it has almost always gone from bad to worse when I try to lead my marriage. God didn't design marriage that way.

1 Peter 3:6 mentions Sarah as our example, so let's look at her marriage. Sarah had challenges in her marriage. Abraham, her husband, wanted a

son but she had been unable to get pregnant. I imagine that Abraham was all fired up about God's promise that they would have a son (Genesis 15:4). Sarah probably felt a lot of pressure when month after month, she did not get pregnant. After ten years of waiting for this promise to be fulfilled (Genesis 16:1-3), Sarah gives way to her fear and takes control of the situation. She tells her husband to sleep with her servant. (Sarah must have hit bottom at this point.) She reasons that perhaps she can have a family through her servant.

Instead of solving her problem, that decision multiplied her problems. It would be another thirteen years of waiting, and by then Sarah's womb was dead (Romans 4:19). But God then blessed Abraham and Sarah with a son, and somewhere along the way, she learned to totally trust God and her husband. I believe the silence in the scriptures about any reaction from Sarah when God later tested Abraham by telling him to sacrifice their son Isaac (Genesis 22) is a tribute to her trust in God and her husband at that point in her life. She didn't step in and take control from Abraham. She wasn't giving way to fear anymore. God holds her up as an example for us as a woman who made herself beautiful in his eyes by submitting to her husband. God calls us to follow her example.

I appreciate how realistic the Bible is. It is not a fairy tale about people who are larger than life, but it is about people with real struggles, like Sarah. She struggled the same as you and me and overcame her fear by faith. She became the example for us in not giving way to fear. It took her awhile – she was over 90 years old before she became a mother and saw her faith answered by God! Hopefully, we won't have to wait that long since we have her example to follow. But no matter what your age or how long you have been married, God is calling you to overcome any fear you may have of submission.

Single women can face many fears about submission, also. A common response (whether single or married) is to try to take control of the men in our lives. If you are dating someone, and you want to build a close friendship, you will need to overcome your fears about submission. Of course, as a single woman, you are not under the leadership of your boyfriend as a wife is her husband, but you may still find it difficult to trust his leadership.

In the book of Ruth, we read about Orpah, a young widow. She was Naomi's other daughter-in-law. Consider how she dealt with her fears. In the first chapter of Ruth, when Orpah's prospects for another marriage seemed dim, she feared she would not have another husband so she left Naomi and God. There were two wealthy kinsmen-redeemers (eligible bachelors) at the end of the book of Ruth (Ruth 3:12), but Orpah was not around because she had gone back to Moab. God had a plan for her life, but her fears took her in another direction.

Do you give way to fear? Think back about your last disagreement with your husband (or boyfriend). What was it about? Were you trying to get him to do something he didn't think was important? Why were you disagreeing with him? Were you motivated in some way by fear? Did he say something that stirred up a fear within you of being controlled or hurt in some way?

As I have discussed the topic of fear with other women, several have told me they don't argue out of fear. One friend told me she was angry instead of fearful. I asked her why she was angry in her last disagreement with her husband. She said that she was angry because she thought that what he was doing was not good for their children. I helped her see that she was afraid something was going to hurt their children. It may be displayed as anger, but the anger was out of fear. That was how she dealt with her fear – she became angry and forceful.

If you think your husband is making a mistake, how do you respond to him? Do you get angry? Do you argue with him? Do you take over the leadership and start bossing him? I think it is helpful to do a little self-analysis to find out what is the real fear. If I can understand what my fear is, I find it helpful in letting go of my unrighteous response.

For instance, have you ever fought over directions while driving somewhere? Were you thinking that you would be late, or did you think you knew a better way to go? What happens if you are late because he did not take the fastest route? Are you afraid it reflects badly on you?

Personally, I dislike being tardy. I also dislike driving fast to get somewhere because we are late. My husband is very busy and usually tries to get more done than time allows. He often leaves the house later than he planned, and occasionally he gets engrossed in conversation and misses his exit. You can see our potential for conflict regarding this! We had many arguments about being late, but I could not change this in my husband. This is an area I have had to completely surrender to God. It helped me to let go of trying to control this when I thought through the worst-case scenario. Most of the time, the result is insignificant. We are often a few minutes late, but so what if we are? I would rather be late than be bossy with my husband and have him feel disrespected by me. What I did do was make many of our rides tense. So now I often arrive a few minutes late, but we have a peaceful ride there.

Maybe you find that your disagreements are generally about the same thing. Are you afraid of something? I've found fears that stir within me that cause me to disagree with my husband in certain situations. After I identify my fear, I can deal with it more effectively.

It's helpful to see the impact of our fears. We can do some crazy things out of fear. Are you afraid of what other people think? I've seen women correct their husbands' speech, manners, food selections or other actions while in public because they were concerned about what someone else might think of them. Are you more concerned about what a stranger might think of you than what your husband thinks?

What about the times when there are more significant consequences? For instance, one friend was disagreeing with her husband about their contribution to the church during a very difficult time for them financially. He was not tithing and that went against her convictions. They fought for several days and many harsh and threatening words were said by both of them. Is forcefulness the answer? Her concern was to please God, but without purity, God won't be pleased.

Another friend was distraught because her husband did not have a good relationship with their teenage son. She had collected a list of things her husband wasn't doing right. There was so much tension between the wife and husband that they wouldn't even stay in the same room together. I tried to explain to her how destructive it would be for her son to live in that atmosphere in their home. We have to start with the things we can control. It would have been more beneficial for her son to live in a happy home, even if his relationship with his dad was lacking in some way, than in a home where his mom was miserable because she was unsuccessfully trying to change her husband. There are many pitfalls in trying to change your husband.

We can pay a high price for giving way to our fear. Sarah decided that her servant should have Abraham's child. Can you imagine the impact that decision had on the closeness and intimacy of her marriage? She multiplied her problems, and then blamed Abraham for everything (Genesis 16:5).

Many women I have spoken with say that their husbands won't lead so they have to. I tell them it is like letting someone open a door for you – you sometimes have to pause until they get there. There are several reasons why men won't lead. One is that their wives are impatient and won't give them enough time. I can quickly decide what needs to happen, but it is not my place to lead Jim, and I don't have to figure it out for him. (I can also quickly make a bad decision.)

Another reason is when a husband is so opposed by his wife at every turn that he gives up and retreats from trying to lead. Some men will retreat to idleness, such as television or entertainment, others to their career or sports, and some men retreat to the busyness of the ministry. In other words, he quits leading. Is that godly? No, but the other choice isn't great either – he can fight it out with you! If he is a conflict avoider, it is unlikely he will do that.

If you oppose his leadership, he may become insecure. He needs to know you are merciful if he makes a mistake. So what if he makes a mistake? Haven't you made a few mistakes yourself? I have. Fortunately, most of the time they can be corrected. I just try again with a little more experience. Again, it's helpful to understand what you are afraid of if he makes a mistake.

Another reason he may be unwilling to lead is criticism. It's hard to do something if you are criticized at every turn. One area in which I have strong opinions is how to get a good bargain. So when Jim and I bought or sold cars or anything else, I would watch Jim and then criticize him afterward. "Why didn't you offer less?" "Why didn't you take that deal? You won't get another one like that."

You can imagine that this was not a good dynamic for us. After one occasion, he looked at me and said, "It would be a lot easier if I were dealing with only one person." I got his point. I certainly didn't want to be a thorn in his negotiations. In my pride, I somehow thought I knew better. But even if I had better negotiating skills, forcefulness was not the answer. My criticism was hurting him.

We can make it difficult for our husbands to lead and then wonder what's their problem. Even if he is a reluctant leader, if you refrain from jumping in and taking over, he will eventually get the job done.

John Gray gives his perspective in his book *Men are From Mars, Women Are From Venus*:

> Generally speaking, when a woman offers unsolicited advice or tries to "help" a man, she has no idea of how critical and unloving she may sound to him. Even though her intent is loving, her suggestions do offend and hurt.[20]

It's important to listen to a man's perspective. We are a helper (*ezer*), but what kind of help does he need? He needs your love and support more than your instructions on how to lead. He needs your help, but that help should first come in the form of joyfully and respectfully following his lead. Nothing else could show him more support or be more helpful.

Your role as a wife or helper to your husband is not to go about pointing out his disobedience, weaknesses or mistakes, nor is it your place to improve him. A wise friend once told me that work is reserved for the Holy Spirit, not the wife. My friend whose husband was not tithing was afraid it put her in a bad relationship with God, and out of fear, she became very forceful and ungodly with her husband. 1 Peter 3:1 says to win your husband over without words by your pure and reverent behavior – not forcefulness.

When a wife is controlling and forceful, her husband feels disrespected, and she often feels lonely. I have felt this loneliness, and Jim has had times when he felt disrespected. His most frequent complaint to me over the years of our marriage was that he did not feel respected. I had no clue what he was talking about, because I thought I did respect him. I did not see these issues of control as a lack of respect.

To become a daughter of Sarah, besides not giving way to fear, we must choose to do what is right. That is something I can control – my own actions! But it is tempting to focus on my husband's shortcomings rather than mine. But that isn't what I am called to do as a daughter of Sarah. I have found that if I will get my focus off of my husband and serve God in a pure and reverent way, I'm much happier. I also have a greater influence with my husband.

Sometimes I want my husband to be strong spiritually so I don't have to work hard at being a Christian. That is ideal and it does make it easier when my husband is doing well spiritually; however, there may be times when he isn't, and God wants me to stay on my course.

If things are not going well in my marriage, my first line of defense is to evaluate how I'm doing in my role. Am I putting a lot of pressure on my husband by somehow giving way to fear? Am I doing what is right? When I step back and do a little self-evaluation, I almost always have something I can work on. But even if I don't see anything I need to work on, if I will give my husband a little time, it always gets worked out.

I've had discussions with wives who wanted someone to talk with their husbands because they thought their husbands were not doing well spiritually. My response was to try to help the wife evaluate how she was reacting to her husband. Often she was distraught and unhappy with her husband because he wouldn't listen to her, or she was emotionally down because he wasn't being "spiritual." So now he was not only facing the first problem that was causing him discouragement or faithlessness, but on top of that, his wife was now upset with him. Many of these wives found that if they would turn up the encouragement and focus on being more loving to their husbands, it all worked out. This is truly a time you can be his *ezer* (someone who comes through for him in a desperate time).

Choosing to do what is right is not usually our first reaction. Our emotions or fears push us in the other direction. This is where a gentle and quiet spirit helps us. We have an inner strength to focus on the right thing and a peacefulness that comes from knowing God is in control – not us.

Worksheet 11 – Sarah's Daughters

1. Do you fear submitting to your husband's leadership? If so, what are your greatest fears about submitting to him?

2. What was your last disagreement about with him?

3. Was it motivated by a fear in you? If so, was it a rational fear? What is the worst-case scenario if your fear came true?

4. What impact did the disagreement have on your husband?

5. Does your husband retreat from leadership? If so, do you feel you must lead in his place? What impact is this having on your relationship? What will it take for you to step back and let him lead?

6. Write a prayer asking God for strength to overcome any fear you may have of your husband's leadership.

Do not be anxious about anything, but in everything, by prayer and petition, with thanksgiving, present your requests to God. — Philippians 4:6

- Chapter 5 -

Why Me?

Does the thought of making changes cause you to struggle? Are you thinking, "Why do I have to change? Why not my husband? After all he is the leader – he should be leading the way in changing too!"

Some of my friends believe the biggest problem in their marriage is their husbands' behavior, not theirs. I'm not disagreeing with them. Some of their husbands need to change, but what will change them? Does nagging, arguing or forcefulness change him, or does it just make you both miserable? I think it is wonderful how God has empowered us as women. He asks us to be humble, pure and reverent, which on the outside may look like a weak position, but in reality God gives us this incredible influence. If you want to make progress, you have to change what you can. Give God something to bless by faithfully following the Bible.

During most of the times that I was trying to change as a wife, my husband wasn't saying, "Let's change together." That made it more difficult, because I knew he had things he could work on. (It's easier to work on his problems than mine!) So my prayer times were critical for me. They helped me get my eyes off of my husband and focus on my own weaknesses.

One of my biggest obstacles was that I didn't think it was fair. But as I would pray and meditate, I would try to imagine what Jesus might say to me about my "it's-not-fair" doctrine. I would imagine myself standing at the cross of Jesus and telling him that it's not fair. Jesus would respond to me by saying that he was not on the cross because of fairness. And he would tell me to take up my cross and follow him. The cross has a tremendous impact on my hard heart. In my early years as a disciple, I was taught that I needed to go to the cross for strength when I was in a spiritual battle. I try to make it as real in my mind as I can, imagining myself standing there having a conversation with Jesus as he bears my punishment. It always puts my problems into perspective and gives me the strength I need.

During some of my most discouraging times, I told God I wasn't leaving my prayer time until he filled me with happiness. That sounds demanding of me, but it was more of a demand on myself rather than God, because I was the one who had to change. It was a time of wrestling with my emotions. God has always answered those prayers. Psalm 31:7 says, "I will be glad and rejoice in your love, for you saw my affliction and knew the anguish of my soul." I believe that joyfulness is a great indicator of true surrender to God. I would continue on with my day with a happy heart. I was determined I would be godly and, if I had sinned, I would make it right with Jim.

There is a great temptation to try to focus on my husband instead of myself, but that is not God's plan for me in changing my marriage. He says to win my husband over without words by the purity and reverence of *my* life.

Remember that being afraid is not the problem. The problem is giving way to it. It is important to deal with the things you are afraid of. There are some effective ways to do that.

Pray & Fast

One is prayer – turn it over to God. Your prayers say a lot about you. I have learned through my experiences that if I will pray to God before I talk to others, I will be in much better shape emotionally.

What do you pray for? Are you praying, "Lord, change my husband," or "Lord, change me."? I have often prayed for my husband to change and God answered some of those prayers, but as I have gotten older, I pray more often for me to change. Sometimes I am driven to pray because of problems, but it's a higher goal to pray about what I can change. That is something I can control!

Another way to get help with problems is to fast. **(Some women I know can't fast because of health problems, so check with your doctor if you aren't sure about your health.)** If you can't fast from food because of health issues, choose something to fast from that will have a big impact on your lifestyle. As I have discussed marriage problems with many women, I have found few women who have ever fasted for their marriage. Fasting has been an effective way to help me let go of bitterness, discouragement or fears. I pray for spiritual strength during my fasts. I usually fast from food from sundown to sundown and drink only water. If it's a work day, I may drink some juice.

When I first began fasting, I found it very difficult. My spiritual muscles were weak, and I had a difficult time saying no to myself. Also, my diet was not very healthy and I lacked self-control. (It's harder to fast when you eat a lot of junk food.) It seems like most days that I've fasted when I had to go to work, someone at my office would bring me a piece of homemade cake and insist I try it and tell them if I liked it. Once I gave in to that. Other times I've said thanks and left the cake on my desk all day long. At first I wanted to keep food out of sight because of the temptation, but I began to see a clear picture of my weakness and how easily I was swayed. I was losing the battle with Satan. That riled me up and gave me more stamina. I came to the conviction that even if I were surrounded by food, I wouldn't eat it. My spiritual muscles have grown stronger.

Hunger is one of the most powerful forces in your life and saying no to hunger can help you grow in saying no to other difficult things, such as saying no to your emotions and saying no to sin. Fasting can strengthen you. It's not a tool to manipulate God, but a time to humble yourself and ask for his strength and guidance. Consider this passage in Isaiah 58 about fasting:

> *"Is not this the kind of fasting I have chosen: to loose the chains of injustice and untie the cords of the yoke, to set the oppressed free and break every yoke? Is it not to share your food with the hungry and to provide the poor wanderer with shelter— when you see the naked, to clothe him, and not to turn away from your own flesh and blood? Then your light will break forth like the dawn, and your healing will quickly appear; then your righteousness will go before you, and the glory of the LORD will be your rear guard. Then you will call, and the LORD will answer; you will cry for help, and he will say: Here am I. If you do away with the yoke of oppression, with the pointing finger and malicious talk, and if you spend yourselves in behalf of the hungry and satisfy the needs of the oppressed, then your light will rise in the darkness, and your night will become like the noonday. The LORD will guide you always; he will satisfy your needs in a sun-scorched land and will strengthen your frame. You will be like a well-watered garden, like a spring whose waters never fail."*
>
> *Isaiah 58:6-11*

One of my goals as I have fasted for my marriage was to do away with "the pointing finger and malicious talk." Verse 11 describes how I want to see my marriage: "a well-watered garden, like a spring whose waters never fail."

I have fasted one day a week for a period of time, going back to God again and again in prayer until I made progress. When I've prayed for guidance, God has always answered that prayer quickly. I prayed for guidance one morning and that night a friend recommended a book to me. I went home that night and ordered the book. That book taught me a lot. It was an answered prayer. We must turn to God and ask him to help us.

I have made progress, but there are still times I see my shortcomings as a wife. Purity of heart is my greatest challenge. There are times when I know what I should do, and I do it, but not from my heart. That is not a fun way to live. So how do you get your heart to follow your actions? What I have found is that I must fast and pray when my heart won't follow. I do not want to go through the motions and submit to my husband out of duty. I want to have a pure heart and obey God joyfully as I live the life of a disciple of Jesus. This works for me in every aspect of my life, whether it is submitting to my husband's leadership, forgiving someone or sharing my faith. It is not acceptable to me to go through the motions, because I know I will be discouraged without a heartfelt motivation as I obey God. So I have fasted and prayed, asking God to help me change my heart. God wants to give us a new heart.

> *I will give you a new heart and put a new spirit in you; I will remove from you your heart of stone and give you a heart of flesh.*
>
> *Ezekiel 36:26*

Remember Mercy

Growing in my understanding of God's mercy has also helped me during discouraging times. I have found that there are two obstacles that many of us face in our efforts to become gentle and quiet. The first one is to see the truth about these qualities. They describe a strong and peaceful woman, not someone who is weak or passive. However, if you get past the first obstacle and you now want these qualities in your life, you will find that they are not easy to acquire. That's where we face the second obstacle: the temptation to think that these are unattainable. I threw this book away three times while writing it because I felt like a hypocrite. I was tempted to give up. Inner strength and peace do not come easily. And when something isn't easy, there may be a tendency to give up the goal. That's where God's mercy can help us.

> *Let us then approach the throne of grace with confidence, so that we may receive mercy and find grace to help us in our time of need.*
>
> *Hebrews 4:16*

This verse says that we can approach God with confidence in our time of need. But it can be challenging to be confident when you are needy. Nevertheless, God wants us to know that we can be confident of his grace and mercy during these times.

Imagine for a moment that you've been trying to grow in a gentle and quiet spirit and you have lost the battle every day this week. How would you handle that? Would you want to give up and say, "That's just not me. I can't be gentle and quiet."? Or would you go back to God in your time of need and ask for his mercy and feel like you can start again because you have a clean slate?

Personally, I can become discouraged and distressed by my spiritual failures. However, a better understanding of mercy has helped me keep trying. A gentle and quiet spirit is a lofty goal, and it's easy to get down on yourself and give up the spiritual fight. But if you remember that God is merciful, you can keep working toward the goal.

If you struggle with this, don't get down on yourself, but be determined to grow spiritually. Don't give up the fight for these wonderful qualities. It will take time to develop these. If you are experiencing some failures as you try to grow in a gentle and quiet spirit, remember that God is rich in mercy (Ephesians 2:4). It's like having a blank check for mercy that we can use "in our time of need."

God wants us to be rich in mercy too (Matthew 18:21-35). My fear of doing something wrong can overflow into my relationship with Jim. I sometimes worry about him doing something wrong. This can create some tense times between us. Fortunately, God doesn't pull us over like a traffic cop and give us a ticket every time we do something wrong. And if you show up in his court and plead guilty, he dismisses the charge. The only stipulation he has for us is that we show the same kind of compassion to those around us and that would include our husbands.

> *He has showed you, O man, what is good. And what does the LORD require of you? To act justly and to love mercy and to walk humbly with your God.*
>
> *Micah 6:8*

I love mercy! At least, I love receiving it! However, in this verse, he is talking about giving it. Do you love to give mercy to your husband and others? Do you love having that blank check to write out whenever someone needs a little or a lot of mercy?

Continuing to Grow

It is vital you continue to grow and change no matter how long you've been a Christian.

> *For this very reason, make every effort to add to your faith goodness; and to goodness, knowledge; and to knowledge, self-control; and to self-control, perseverance; and to perseverance, godliness; and to godliness, brotherly kindness; and to brotherly kindness, love. For <u>if you possess these qualities in increasing measure</u>, they will keep you from being ineffective and unproductive in your knowledge of our Lord Jesus Christ. [Emphasis added.]*
>
> *2 Peter 1:5-8*

When I first became a disciple, it was more obvious to me what needed to change in my life, so I worked hard to make changes. Generally, my marriage was much happier. But as I have already said, we hit a plateau that we seemed to come back to again and again. We would do well for a while, but then we would hit the same bump again.

During this time of my life, I was praying that God would help me grow spiritually. I had no idea what I needed to change, but God began to show me several areas in my relationship with Jim that needed spiritual growth. During that year there were times when I was overwhelmed by my sin, but I kept reminding myself of my prayer. God gave me the strength to make some deep character changes. It is very exhilarating to change for God. Acts 3:19 says that times of refreshing will come after repentance. I have experienced those times of refreshing. God also says that he will lift you up if you humble yourself before him (James 4:10).

Consider how the qualities mentioned in 2 Peter 1:5-8 impact you in regard to your marriage and why it is important to continue to grow in them.

Faith: You may be struggling to have faith in God's plan for marriage, or you may have little faith that your marriage will ever change. You may even be faithful in other areas of your life, but for some reason you struggle to believe your marriage will grow. Faith makes a big difference in how we approach our challenges. Remember our faith is in God and his power, not in ourselves.

Goodness: You may need to grow in goodness toward your husband and stop saying and doing unrighteous things.

Knowledge: You may need to grow in your knowledge of the scriptures and learn God's plan instead of being pulled in by fine-sounding ideas Hollywood is broadcasting.

Self-control: Self-control is useful in restraining your words, and it will also help you rein in your emotions.

Perseverance: Perseverance will help you through a tough time.

Godliness: Godliness means you become more like God. God is holy. He is never bitter or unforgiving. If you are going to be godly, you have to get rid of any bitterness toward your husband and love showing mercy. There are many godly qualities that we can add to our marriage.

Kindness: Kindness is a soothing quality in a marriage. Are you growing in kindness toward your husband?

Love: Love is the crown jewel of this passage. There is no better place to grow in love than with the man you have pledged your love to with a solemn oath on your wedding day.

Two verses before this passage we find this statement: "His divine power has given us everything we need for life and godliness." We have everything we need to be godly in our marriage. Verse 8 says that if we have these qualities in increasing measure, we will be effective and productive. Next time you are in the middle of a challenge in your marriage, ask yourself which of these qualities you need. Is it faithfulness, perseverance, love, etc.? God wants to bless you with these qualities, and he wants you to make every effort to add them to your life.

If you are married, your marriage is really where the rubber meets the road in your walk with God. It's the greatest display of your walk with God. This is a high calling, isn't it? But God will help you because he wants you to succeed. I am amazed at how God has blessed my life and marriage as I have sought to grow in these areas. I do not boast about this from a standpoint of what I've done. I boast in the Lord because he is able to do what he has promised.

God designed this incredible relationship he calls marriage. He gave us our role as a wife. We must trust that he loves us and values us. He wants to bless us!

I continue to try to grow in my love and respect for my husband. I love what God has done in my marriage. I want to encourage you to dig deep and pray often and change what you can. The rewards are great.

Worksheet 12 – Making Changes

> *It's the most unhappy people who most fear change.*
> — Mignon McLaughlin

1. How long have you been a Christian?

2. Do you actively pursue spiritual growth?

3. In which area of your marriage would you like to see growth or change?

4. Have you ever fasted for your marriage?

5. Do you pray about any disagreements you have with your husband?

6. Are you quick to ask for mercy when you need it?

7. Read Micah 6:8. Do you love showing mercy to your husband?

8. Which of the qualities listed in 2 Peter 1:5-8 (faith, goodness, knowledge, self-control, perseverance, godliness, kindness or love) would benefit you the most in your marriage at this time? Write a prayer asking God to help you grow in that quality.

Be. . .faithful in prayer.
Romans 12:12

- Chapter 6 -

Self-Evaluation

How do we grow in purity and reverence and how do we develop a gentle and quiet spirit? Can I just say a few prayers and fast for a couple of days? For years in my marriage, I tried hard to respect my husband, but he didn't always feel respected. I needed some practical help. Following are some questions that I have found helpful in evaluating where I am in my relationship with my husband. These questions help me determine if I am staying within my role and willingly following my husband's leadership. They help me evaluate whether I am trying to control my husband in some way. The questions overlap somewhat and they build on each other. After I evaluate where I am, I can see if there is an area in which I need to be more surrendered.

Remember that a wife with a gentle and quiet spirit is surrendered first to God and then to her husband's leadership. It's important to remember the things you have studied regarding a pure and reverent life. Without a pure motivation of pleasing God, it will be difficult to make progress. I want to encourage you to ask yourself these questions and, perhaps, discuss your answers with a close, spiritual friend.

Do I "boss" my husband?

Wives, submit to your husbands as to the Lord.
Ephesians 5:22

You are bossy if you command your husband to do things. Bossiness is one of the most obvious forms of "control." It is the opposite of submissive.

Are you bossy? You may be a bossy wife and not even know it. Some of my bossiest girlfriends don't think they are bossy. I suggest you watch old television shows like *Home Improvement* or *Everybody Loves Raymond,* looking for anything the wife does that is bossy or disrespectful. Movies are also a good resource for this exercise, for example, *Moonstruck* or *My Cousin Vinny.* When I watched these movies with my girlfriends, we laughed the loudest when we saw ourselves in the characters. Bossiness is more obvious when you see it in someone else.

Do you use commanding phrases as you discuss things with your husband? Do you say things like "You should…" or "Why don't you…?" Once you get tuned in to bossiness, you will see it everywhere! Here are some "commands" I've heard wives give their husbands:

At a party: "Tell the kids not to do that anymore."

At the grocery store: "Don't get that brand."

At church service: "Let's go right now."

At a friend's house: "Bring the dog inside."

I have said similar things. I can be a little commander. Take the trash out, let's get going, do this, get that, go here, etc. Acting like the commander-in-chief can create a very bad dynamic in your household. That is not the role God gave you, and it sets a terrible example for your children and everyone around you.

You will pay a price for bossing your husband. Men do not want to be bossed by their wives. They either respond with angry words and frustration or with indifference. He may retreat from leading and let his wife take charge of the affairs of the household. Bossing your husband can take you both out of your God-given roles and do a lot of other damage to your marriage.

If you routinely boss your husband, you may find it hard to stop. It will take a lot of inner strength (the gentle spirit) to overcome the thoughts and feelings behind it. You will need to dig out any fears you have that may be behind your bossiness.

To overcome bossiness, a good place to start is by not saying a word! Learn to think before you speak. You may even need to pray and fast to overcome this. You may be thinking, "But he needs me to tell him what to do," or "He won't do anything if I don't tell him what to do." Remember Uzzah – don't touch it. It's not your place to lead or boss your husband. Get in touch with your fears and step out of the role of "boss."

A gentle and quiet spirit will help you stay in your role. *Praus* (gentle) describes a strong woman who is submitted to God's leadership and her husband's leadership. *Hesuchios* (quiet) describes a woman who is peaceful.

Remember that this has nothing to do with your importance or his importance. The marriage relationship is a very special relationship, and staying within your role will create more intimacy. You show trust by not bossing, and trust is a huge expression of love (1 Corinthians 13:7).

Worksheet 13 – Overcoming Bossiness

> *Most women set out to change a man, and when they have changed him they do not like him.*
> — Marlene Dietrich

1. Is there an area in which you boss your husband? If so, what impact does it have on your husband when you are bossy?

2. If you find you are bossy, ask yourself why. Are you reacting to a fear that you have?

3. During the next 24 hours, as you speak with your husband, notice if you boss him in any way. Keep a list of the areas in which you tend to be bossy so you can pray about letting go of your bossiness.

Ask and it will be given to you; seek and you will find . . .

Matthew 7:7

Are my expectations demanding?

Expectations are another form of control. This kind of control can happen without words but still be demanding. This is when a wife has an expectation that her husband must either live up to or pay a price. If their date or her birthday party or their anniversary trip does not go the way she wants, she puts him in the doghouse. He knew what she wanted but didn't meet her expectations, so she withdraws from him and is moody.

I've seen some very emotional responses to unmet expectations. "He doesn't think I'm important." "He doesn't consider my needs." "He doesn't love me." Sometimes the words were expressed with tears, sometimes anger. Consider this verse:

> *The leech has two daughters. "Give! Give!" they cry.*
> *Proverbs 30:15*

If you tell him what he has to give you or what he must do for you, and then he gives you what you want or does what you told him to do, you won't know if he acted out of love or did his duty to keep the peace. I would rather have a gift Jim picked out for me than one that I forced him to buy to keep me happy. And how happy can I be if I think he only bought it to stay out of the doghouse? How unfulfilling! If it's not a gift from his heart, will I ever feel truly loved?

I'm not saying don't tell him what you like, but there is a big difference between "what I like" and "you have to do this or I will be upset." In the latter case, you may get the gift you want but do a lot of damage to the intimacy of your relationship.

Sometimes my husband asks me what I want for a special occasion. I usually give him a couple of ideas, but I especially love it when he comes up with an idea totally out of the blue. On some occasions he is not very creative, but at other times he sweeps me off my feet. Being grateful for what he does for me, even if it isn't my first choice, is a great way to encourage his creativity. It also brings us closer.

Worksheet 14 – Letting Go of Expectations

1. Do you try to orchestrate what your husband gives to you or does for you? If so, do you get upset if he doesn't meet your expectation?

2. Do special days of celebration cause tension in your marriage?

3. Do you frequently express gratitude to your husband for the little things he does for you?

Are my words gracious?

He who loves a pure heart and whose speech is gracious will have the king for his friend.

Proverbs 22:11

From the fruit of his lips a man is filled with good things as surely as the work of his hands rewards him.

Proverbs 12:14

Our words draw us together or drive us apart. Proverbs 12:14 says it well – your words can fill your life with good things. In Chapter 3 we looked at Queen Esther's example of gracious speech and the impact it had on her life. Jesus is also a great example of someone who spoke gracious words.

All spoke well of him and were amazed at the gracious words that came from his lips. "Isn't this Joseph's son?" they asked.

Luke 4:22

There are many amazing things about Jesus' life – his love for people, the miracles he performed, and his resurrection from the dead. But Jesus' speech was also amazing because his words were gracious. Gracious speech is amazing, and it has a powerful effect on those who hear it. Are you amazing anyone with your gracious speech?

Becoming more gracious in my speech had a very positive effect on my marriage. Graciousness impacts the way I respond and the way I make a request.

An important aspect of graciousness is how you communicate your needs. You may be wondering how you are going to get any help around the house if you are not going to boss your husband anymore. The answer is to speak more graciously.

Many times I have wanted my husband to figure out what it was that I needed. I thought it meant that he was somehow more connected and a better husband – it showed how much he cared about me. It was one of those Hollywood ideas! Anyway, I spent some sad moments because he never did get it. By the time I would tell him, I usually had built up a bad attitude, and he would respond defensively because he felt attacked. I have found that if I will graciously let him know my request, he will do what he can to fulfill it. This is more evidence to me that a husband has a natural inclination to please his wife.

Learning to make a gracious request instead of bossing can dramatically change the atmosphere in a home.

> Bossing: "Honey, the trash is full. Take it out."

> Graciousness: "Honey, can you take out the trash?"

Another part of graciousness is the tone you use. Tone has as much to do with graciousness as the words themselves.

> Sarcastic tone: "Honey, would it be *too much* for you to take out the trash?"

> Impatient tone: "Honey, (sigh) would you be able to take out the trash?"

Sometimes when we are expecting guests, my husband will ask me how he can help. He may even say, "Tell me what I can do to help." But even then I still try to put it in the form of a request.

We have busy lives and it's easy to step into bossiness when we feel pressured. Graciousness will build a much better atmosphere than bossiness. You may still feel the pressure of getting everything done, but you will have a happier atmosphere in which to live. Gracious speech has great rewards.

Worksheet 15 – Gracious Speech

> *Positive Reinforcement is hugging your husband when he does a load of laundry. Negative Reinforcement is telling him he used too much detergent.* -Dr. Joyce Brothers

Consider each of these verses in light of your speech with your husband:

1. Proverbs 16:24 - Would you characterize the words you say to your husband as sweet? Who are you most apt to speak to in a sweet tone?

2. Proverbs 17:27 - Can you restrain the words you speak when you disagree with your husband?

3. 1 Thessalonians 5:18 - Do you let your husband know how grateful you are for the things he does for you or the gifts he gives you?

4. James 3:17 - Do you speak with wisdom? Would the words "pure, peace-loving, considerate, submissive, full of mercy, impartial and sincere" describe your conversations with your husband?

5. Proverbs 12:18 - Do you think before you speak?

6. Ephesians 4:29 - Does your husband generally feel encouraged by you?

7. When does your husband need encouragement the most? Do you find it difficult to encourage him during that time?

8. In which of the areas mentioned in 1 through 6 above do you need to grow the most?

9. Read David's prayer in Psalm 19:14 and write a prayer about your words being pleasing to God.

. . .knock and the door will be opened to you.

Matthew 7:7

95

Are my emotions controlling me?

> *For the grace of God that brings salvation has appeared to all men. It teaches us to say "No" to ungodliness and worldly passions, and to live self-controlled [sophronos], upright and godly lives in this present age...*
>
> Titus 2:11-12

Our emotions, although an awesome part of our being, are a great challenge to living a "self-controlled, upright and godly" life.

The Greek word translated "self-control" in the above verse is *sophronos.*

> **Definition:** *Sophronos* (so-fron'-oce) safe (sound) in mind, moderate as to opinion or passion, discreet, temperate.[21] It suggests the exercise of self-restraint that governs all passions and desires, enabling the believer to be conformed to the mind of Christ.[22]

Self-control involves restraining not only our actions but also our thinking. Are you safe in what you think about? Is it sound? Do you *allow* bitter, critical or angry thoughts to dwell in your mind?

I've had to battle my own bitter thoughts. I wrote the words of Job 36:13 on several cards: "The godless in heart harbor resentment." I placed them by my phone, by my bed, on my mirror and in my purse. Every time I saw this verse, I checked my heart and mind to see what I was thinking and feeling. I trained myself to be self-controlled or safe in my thinking.

Are you moderate in your opinions and passions or do your emotions control you? Runaway emotions are the opposite of a gentle and quiet spirit. Remember the true definitions of these qualities – power under control and tranquillity arising from within.

The word emotion comes from inner motion. God gave us the ability to feel and to express our feelings. We are not robots. That's good! But when we are driven by our emotions, that's not good.

We can use this emotional force to try to move our husbands. I've heard many wives say, "I just want him to know how I feel." Usually it was when they felt hurt by something their husbands did or didn't do. Your feelings may be too heavy for your husband. He may feel attacked and react defensively. If you are lonely and feeling neglected, you have a couple of ways you can express it. One is, "I feel sad (or mad) because you are not spending enough time with me." The other is, "When can we get some time together? I miss you." Consider the level of respect with these two options. The first one is driven by emotions, but the second one by graciousness.

If you only express how you feel, then he has to guess how to fix it. He may be thinking, "I'm doing all this work on the house trying to please you, and now you don't feel like I'm doing enough for you." In the past I've told my husband that I didn't feel loved. Jim often responded by telling me all the things he had done for me. Instead, if I had graciously asked him if we could spend more time together, he would have better understood what I needed and responded in a more favorable way.

I had to teach my children to express their needs in a respectful way when they were young. Sometimes on a hot day when they had been playing, they would come into the kitchen and declare, "I'm thirsty!" If I didn't stop and get them a drink immediately, they would raise their voices and say indignantly, "I said I'm thirsty!" I call this the "center of the universe" syndrome! The kids tell you their problems, and since they are the center of the universe and everything revolves around them, you are supposed to make them happy. You have to find the solution. Occasionally when I gave them a drink of water, they responded, "I don't want water!" So next I was expected to guess what they were thirsty for. Instead, I would tell them that they needed to ask nicely. So I taught them to say, "Mom, may I have a drink?" I would send them out of the room and tell them to walk back into the room and try it again. Their hearts had to be trained to make a respectful request.

I could easily see this problem in my children, but without thinking about it, I was making my husband guess what I wanted. If your husband has to guess what will make you happy, you may be waiting awhile. If you think it through, you can figure out how to make a gracious request. It's a new way of thinking for many wives. Instead of emotionally presenting what's wrong, you must figure out how you can make a *positive*, *loving* request. Your chances are much better that he will be able to meet your need.

How do we become like this? How can I make a gracious request when I'm feeling emotional? Titus 2:11-12 says that God's grace will teach us to say no to passions and ungodliness. Now, God isn't saying, "Just say no," like the drug slogan today. Instead, he wants us to be motivated from our hearts by his favor in our lives. His favor can be a powerful motivation.

His favor motivates me. There are times when my emotions are overtaking me and I'm feeling anxious. One remedy I have for those times is to stop and force myself to smile! Yes, smile! There is something very relaxing about a smile – a real smile. I still have a lot to smile about in my life even when things aren't going smoothly. Jesus has given me a lot to smile about. I try to focus for a moment on those things by getting a broader view than just the moment I'm living in. The following verses are two of my favorite "smile" verses:

> *To him who is able to keep you from falling and to present you before his glorious presence without fault and with great joy.*
>
> *Jude 1:24*

> *However, as it is written: "No eye has seen, no ear has heard, no mind has conceived what God has prepared for those who love him."*
>
> *1 Corinthians 2:9*

Don't those verses make you smile? If you didn't smile as you read them, you didn't let the truth of them sink into your heart. These verses are speaking of God's favor and what that favor means in your life. Jude 1:24 is telling us that in spite of all our weaknesses, he will be able to present us without fault and with great joy. 1 Corinthians 2:9 is telling us about an incredible, unbelievable reward God has prepared for us. If you were told you just won the state lottery, would that change your disposition? These verses are telling you something far better than winning the lottery.

My point is that we have more control over our emotions than we realize. Have you ever been in a heated discussion with someone when the phone rang, and you picked it up and said hello in a completely different tone of voice? Why do we do that? Because it is not the time or place to let go of our emotions. So we *can* take control of our emotions.

After I have gotten my smile on, I look at my husband with my smile. I know he is encouraged when I smile at him – a real smile! I can see him melt a little, especially if we are in a hectic or tense moment in our schedule. After this little attitude adjustment time, I find that I can be encouraging even when things aren't running as smoothly as I would like.

An illustration that has helped me get control of my inner motion is a transportation example. It's like the difference in riding on a fast-moving train and a fast-moving airplane. If you look out of the window at the ground while riding on a fast train, it can make you spin. Your emotions can be just like that – they can make you spin. But even though you are going faster in an airplane, if you look out at the ground, it seems you are hardly moving, because you are 30,000 feet higher. You are looking at a much broader view. If I can catch my emotions for a moment and consider what I am doing, I ask myself, "Will this really matter in 100 years?" (That's the airplane view of my life at that moment.) That question will help me get control of my emotions. Of course, I won't be living on this earth in 100 years, so it helps me to get a spiritual perspective of my life at that moment and see what really matters. I can often say that it probably won't matter in ten years (or one year).

Many years ago the first time I caught myself like this was a day I was driving my car fast as I was doing my errands. I was in a hurry and full of tension. It dawned on me how God must be seeing me at that moment like a hurried little ant running in a circle. It made me laugh and take a deep breath. I slowed down. I was able to get rid of the inner "motion."

Over the years my emotions have taken me on many "train" rides. I've been emotional over some serious things but also over some trivial things. A spiritual perspective always helps me. I try to help my friends see the bigger picture of their lives when we are discussing their problems. They might be in a very difficult time, but looking at the bigger picture still helps them. We talk about the worst thing that might happen at this time, but overall in 100 years what will they be thinking?

So next time the kids color on the wall, your husband mows down your new flowers, both of your cars break down on the same day, or when you have received bad news about something, try to get a broader picture. It will help you stay steady in your faith. The following verse says it well:

> *Therefore we do not lose heart. Though outwardly we are wasting away, yet inwardly we are being renewed day by day. For our light and momentary troubles are achieving for us an eternal glory that far outweighs them all. So we fix our eyes not on what is seen, but on what is unseen. For what is seen is temporary, but what is unseen is eternal.*
> *2 Corinthians 4:16-18*

When I read about the apostle Paul's life, I do not think of the troubles he faced as "light and momentary." He faced all kinds of serious troubles, but he had a spiritual perspective that helped him face them faithfully.

You and I need this same spiritual perspective. It will help you to slow down the "motion" and become more gracious. You will then be able to show more kindness, courtesy, gratitude, compassion, etc. Growing in these qualities could bring about much more romance for many couples.

Worksheet 16 – Controlling Your Emotions

1. Are you known for being emotional?

2. Can you restrain yourself in the middle of an emotional time?

3. What emotions do you most easily give in to?

4. What helps you the most to gain self-control over your emotions?

5. Read 1 Peter 1:13. Write a prayer asking God to help you grow in your self-control.

Therefore be clear minded and self-controlled so that you can pray.

1 Peter 4:7

Do I treat him like one of the kids?

...and the wife must respect her husband.

Ephesians 5:33

It is not my role to "mother" my husband. This is another form of being bossy, but with a little different flavor. This is when you let your maternal instincts take over. I've heard women say that they have three kids when they actually have only two, because they are including their husbands in the count. It sets up a weird dynamic between a husband and wife when the wife "mothers" her husband. It is very disrespectful and, not surprisingly, it will keep you from developing intimacy in your marriage.

Have you ever heard the saying, "If mom is cold, we all have to wear a sweater."? Picture the child saying, "I'm hot" and the mom saying, "No, it's cold, you wear a sweater." We can do that with our husbands too. Of course, you may need to help a child, but your husband is not a child. He can make his own decision on what to wear. If he gets cold he may decide the next time to take a jacket. I do not tell my husband what to wear or when to get his hair cut or what he should eat. My husband often asks for my input about his clothes or hair. I'm glad to give my opinion, but I don't want to do it in a motherly way.

I have a friend whose husband had health problems, and he had to rest often because of fatigue. She was frustrated because she had so much to do. However, if he offered to do something, she would respond, "No, you are too tired." She then had to do the housework by herself. She was trying to be sensitive, but she was deciding for him when he was too tired. He can make that decision for himself. She learned to accept his help when offered and found she wasn't as stressed.

I have watched a friend argue with her husband about what food he wanted to order while eating out at a restaurant. While at someone's home, I've seen a wife remove steak from her husband's plate after he had served himself, because she thought he should first offer the plate of meat to their guests. She was acting out of embarrassment, but her actions only made things worse. She felt he was being disrespectful to his guests, but she was being very disrespectful to her husband by taking charge of the moment. As their guests, my husband and I really didn't think anything of her husband serving himself first, but her actions changed the atmosphere immediately.

A friend asked me how she could help her husband eat a healthier diet. She was very concerned about his eating habits, and they often disagreed about what he was eating. I asked her if her attempts to change his eating habits were working. She said no. Instead, they usually had a disagreement, and he still ate whatever he wanted. My advice to her was to try to cook healthier meals and have healthier snacks around, but otherwise let it go. She was not accomplishing her goal. It was only making things worse.

I want to distinguish between mothering and pampering. I'm not talking about whether your husband enjoys being pampered. My husband likes to be pampered, but not mothered. I like to be pampered too. Pampering each other is a fun part of our relationship. However, mothering your husband throws a lot of cold water on the intimacy of your relationship. Women have a nurturing side, but we need to keep it in check and make sure we aren't stepping into a "mom" role with our husbands.

As a wife, we sometimes struggle to know what our role is. You want to help, but when you start mothering, you show that you do not understand your husband's deeper needs. At this point in his life, he needs a companion, not a mom, and you need a close intimate relationship with him, not a mother/son relationship. God has designed marriage to be an intimate relationship. Many women long for a closer marriage, but they do not understand how they hurt the intimacy of their relationship. You have a choice. You can focus on making your husband look better and do better, or you can enjoy this great relationship God has given you.

It's helpful to remember that your husband managed somehow before he married you. He got himself dressed, fed and to work every day. He didn't marry you so he would have someone to tell him what to do. God's plan is much better than that. God has set us up for an intimate relationship with our husbands.

Worksheet 17 - Cutting the Apron Strings

> *Why does a woman work ten years to change a man's habits and then complain that he's not the man she married?*   - Barbara Streisand

1. Do you treat your husband like one of the kids?

2. Do you try to control what he eats or wears? If so, does it irritate your husband when you do so?

3. During the next week, note any area in which you "mother" your husband.

Do I fully submit to his leadership?

> *I also want women to dress modestly, with decency and propriety, not with braided hair or gold or pearls or expensive clothes, but with good deeds, appropriate for women who profess to worship God. A woman should learn in quietness and full submission. I do not permit a woman to teach or to have authority over a man; she must be silent. For Adam was formed first, then Eve. And Adam was not the one deceived; it was the woman who was deceived and became a sinner. But women will be saved through childbearing—if they continue in faith, love and holiness with propriety.*
>
> *1 Timothy 2:9-15*

This is one of those land-mine scriptures for us today. I believe this is a scripture that will set you free when you obey it. Verse 11 says we should learn in quietness and full submission. Does that instruction irritate you? If it does, take a deep breath and let it out slowly and please read on.

This is the counterpart to not being bossy. Not bossing is a beginning, but there is still something missing – submission. We need not only to stop bossing our husbands, but we must also be willing to be led by them. As we have already seen in Chapter 3, submission is a way of life for a Christian. This is not just for wives. However, wives have a special calling to submit to their husbands.

I have heard discussions about whether the above scripture was addressing a cultural teaching for the women of that time and, perhaps, some of it is. However, I think it is interesting that Eve is the reason given in verses 13-14 as to why we should learn in full submission. Eve had no cultural limitations in the Garden of Eden. She could not blame her sin on a social culture, her parents or Adam (even though she tried to blame the serpent). I think modern marriages still have the same struggle that Adam and Eve had in their relationship and that Satan is still doing what he can to cause conflict in our marriages.

This is not the only place that the teaching of "full submission" is given in the Bible. Ephesians 5:24 also says to submit to your husband "in everything." It is my goal to be fully submissive to my husband, not just

90%. I am open to what that means and how I can take it higher. I still find areas in which I need to surrender to his leadership.

Now I realize that the idea of being fully submissive may be offensive to some of my readers. I'm not talking about being a robot or throwing away your brain.

"I can't"

There are times when I say, "I can't" to my husband. He is a self-motivated, industrious person. He usually has a packed schedule. Sometimes he gets a little overzealous in scheduling our week, and I have to tell him that I don't think I can do everything he has planned. I have physical limitations because of back problems, and there are times I tell him I can't do something. I try to let him know in a respectful way that I can't do everything he has planned. I don't tell him not to do something. It is not up to me to direct his schedule, but I can say when mine is overloaded.

"I won't"

There are times a wife should say, "No, I won't" to her husband. Sapphira is an example of this (Acts 5:1-10). Her husband, Ananias, asked her to lie about a donation they were making to the church. In Acts 5:9 Peter asks Sapphira, "How could you agree to test the Spirit of the Lord?" Clearly, Peter did not think Sapphira should have agreed to tell this lie. The scriptures are very clear that we must be truthful. Sapphira should have said, "No, I will not lie. I will not lie *to* you or *for* you." Her husband would have seen her purity and reverence before God. She may have saved his life. She certainly would have saved her own (Acts 5:8-9). But remember a no still needs to be framed in a pure and reverent manner. Consider the following verse:

> *Through patience a ruler can be persuaded, and a gentle tongue can break a bone.*
>
> *Proverbs 25:15*

Not submitting to your husband should be a rare occasion in your home, not the norm. If he is messing up in one area, that doesn't mean you have license to ignore his leadership in other areas. Sometimes a wife can become so focused on what she considers to be a flaw in her husband that it spills over into the other areas of their relationship.

There are times when it's more difficult to know when to say no. On occasions my husband told me how I should handle a situation, and I didn't feel good about it. It went against my conscience. We sometimes talked it through until we got to a solution in which we both felt confident. However, if it doesn't go against my conscience, I want to trust my husband and follow his advice. I have found his advice to be very wise when I originally didn't think it was.

There have also been occasions when I did as he suggested but didn't like the outcome. For example, our neighbors had sold their home. I was speaking with this neighbor on the phone when my husband told me to ask her how much they got for it. (We were about to put our house on the market. This was information that would be available through public records in another month or so.) I was hesitant to ask her because I'm more timid than Jim, but I asked anyway because of his request. She told me she wouldn't answer that, because they hadn't closed the deal yet with the buyer. I was embarrassed. After I got off the phone, I told my husband what she said and then I told him that it embarrassed me to ask that question. He sincerely apologized, and we went on with the evening. I believe God smiled at me on that one. I want to be beautiful in God's eyes. I want to be more interested in how God sees me than how a neighbor sees me, and I trust God to work through any flaws in Jim's leadership.

You may be thinking I've gone over the edge with this one. I'm not saying I never disagree with my husband or that I do everything without question. But in my "old" women's lib mind, I thought this kind of submission was a dangerous way to live, because I might be taken advantage of. But actually there has been a nice benefit to my attempt to submit in everything. The trust I now show Jim has helped us become much closer. I have learned to laugh off my old fears and enjoy my relationship with my husband in a greater way.

Besides being fully submissive, 1 Timothy 2:9-15 also mentions our clothing. Verses 9-10 say that we should dress modestly, and then compares wearing expensive things to good deeds. The Greek word translated "expensive" is *poluteles,* the same Greek word which we looked at in Chapter 1. There are only three places in the New Testament where the word *poluteles* is used. The other two are 1 Peter 3:4 and Mark 14:3 (which we looked at in Chapter 1). Remember that *poluteles* means the very end or limit with reference to value. So when he mentions expensive clothing in this passage, he means the *most* expensive clothing. In a similar manner, 1 Peter 3:3-4 also compares outward adornment to inner beauty:

> *Your beauty should not come from outward adornment, such as braided hair and the wearing of gold jewelry and fine clothes. Instead, it should be that of your inner self, the unfading beauty of a gentle and quiet spirit...*
>
> *1 Peter 3:3-4*

Without a doubt, most women love wearing beautiful things! We spend a lot of money on clothes, jewelry, hair, nails and skin care trying to be more beautiful. I have a closet full of clothes – probably enough for several women. But there is another closet full of clothing we need to consider – a closet full of beautiful spiritual garments for us to wear. Wouldn't you like to start your day off by putting on patience or joy like a garment and displaying that quality all day long? With what do you clothe yourself?

> *Awake, awake, O Zion, clothe yourself with strength. Put on your garments of splendor, O Jerusalem, the holy city.*
>
> *Isaiah 52:1*

> *Therefore, as God's chosen people, holy and dearly loved, clothe yourselves with compassion, kindness, humility, gentleness and patience.*
>
> *Colossians 3:12*

I want to be clear on one thing. Looking bad on the outside is not the goal. That won't make you look more beautiful on the inside. We need to look our best. But there is an inner beauty we must also strive for.

We are to be clothed with good deeds appropriate for women who profess to worship God. This includes how you follow the leadership of your husband. People can see what you wear. These deeds need to be as obvious as your clothes. Our respect for our husbands and our willingness to follow their leadership need to be obvious too.

A surrendered wife, who is not spending her time and energy fighting her husband's leadership, can have a more effective ministry for the Lord. I don't believe you have to have a perfect marriage before you can teach other women about the Bible, but your example can speak louder than your words. If a woman is happy in her marriage, she is going to have a greater testimony to share with the women in her neighborhood and workplace. She will be excited about what God is doing in her life.

1 Timothy 2:15 concludes with "women will be saved through child-bearing – if they continue in faith, love and holiness with propriety." We know from other verses in the Bible that childbirth is not a prerequisite of a woman's salvation. However, a woman who is busy with the demands of motherhood may feel like her work is not as valuable as the ministry of someone who has the time to do more. God is letting us know that motherhood is highly valued by him and an important ministry. However, there is a condition placed on this ministry – that she must continue in faith, love and holiness in her walk with God. Motherhood may limit some aspects of a woman's ministry, but not her faith, love and holiness.

It is my goal in being more submitted to my husband that he feels my deepest respect. If he has an idea of how he wants to do something, I say, "sure" or "whatever you think." I offer my help in any way my husband needs. He relies on me a lot to help him with the needs in the church and for ideas in general on how to build a family atmosphere. He also wants my input in the Bible lessons he teaches. He sometimes asks me to study something and give him my thoughts on it. I do not consider our ministries as separate. I think of it as one ministry that he leads in which I am his helper (*ezer*). If he moves one way, I am by his side. If he decides to go another direction, I am there with him. It is okay with me if he changes his mind. My goal is to tell my husband my concerns about things but not from a standpoint of commanding or bossing him.

Many of the conflicts I've experienced in the past were because I was not submissive to Jim's leadership. I was trying to lead the relationship. As a young wife, I was far from being "fully" submissive. I was more in the minus column of submission than the plus column. Even five years ago, putting the "fully" into my vocabulary was a challenge. It was a new way of thinking. The only way I was able to do so was by my reverence for God. I want to please God, but there is no way I'm going to please God without obeying him (John 14:15).

To my surprise, I found that this is how to grow closer to the man I love. This is the way God created us to live in the marriage relationship. From the time of Adam and Eve, husbands have led the marriage relationship.

> *...Your desire will be for your husband, and he will rule over you.*
>
> *Genesis 3:16*

Also, from the beginning, a wife's desire has been for her husband. My greatest desire in my relationship with my husband has been to be close and connected and to feel loved by him.

What is your deepest desire in your relationship with your husband? What will help you fulfill this desire? Have you been going about it successfully? If you desire to have a close and happy relationship, you must do the things that will nurture the relationship. Many wives sabotage their own goals. They want to be close, but then they don't follow their husbands' leadership. Eve is an example of this. She lived in a perfect place but it still wasn't good enough. Her independence led her to some unhappy times.

As I learned the biblical principle of being "fully" submissive, I found that my relationship with my husband grew closer and more intimate, and I felt protected and loved. There have been many rewards.

Worksheet 18 - Completely Surrendered

1. Read Ephesians 5:24. Do you submit to your husband in everything?

2. In what area of your life could you be more submitted?

3. What is your deepest desire in your relationship with your husband?

4. Do you see any ways in which you sabotage that desire?

5. Do you consider your spiritual beauty as often as you do your physical beauty?

6. Is it obvious to people around you that you follow your husband's leadership?

7. Write a prayer asking God to help you grow in your submission to your husband.

For everyone who asks receives; he who seeks finds...
Matthew 7:8

Do I let him manage our household?

> *He must manage his own family well and see that his children obey him with proper respect. (If anyone does not know how to manage his own family, how can he take care of God's church?)...A deacon must be the husband of but one wife and must manage his children and his household well.*
>
> 1 Timothy 3:4-5, 12

This question is also about submission, but it helps with the perspective of how, when and where. These verses are about men who are qualified to be elders and deacons in the church. But even if your husband is not an elder or deacon, it is a good goal to be a family that can be held up as an example for others. From my study of these scriptures, I have come to view my husband as the manager of our household.

A manager is someone who has authority to direct and influence the operations of what he oversees. There are many aspects of managing a household, and the goal of a loving and harmonious family is challenging.

Jim appreciates my help and leaves a great deal to my decision, but I let him direct any aspect of it he wants. I do my best to make our home run as smoothly as possible, but there is no area that I feel he should stay out of. I welcome his input in any area of my life. There were earlier times when I felt insecure if he would make suggestions, and I would bristle at his "intrusion" in my area of domain. Now I ask more questions. I'm much more secure as I've learned about God's expectations for my role.

Do you let your husband manage your household? One of the greatest obstacles a husband can face in managing his household is that his household refuses to be managed. As a wife, you can make his work impossible. If you won't follow, he can't lead you.

It can be hard to let go of preconceived ideas about how you think he should manage it. Many wives have a set of rules that they believe their husbands must adhere to. If he doesn't do it their way, they won't follow. I've spoken with some women who felt their husbands were not being "spiritual" men. They had their idea of what "spiritual" looked like and when their husbands weren't living up to their definition, they quit following.

There are many ways we can make it difficult for them to lead. Remember the goal is to have a loving and harmonious family. Leadership is vital to the smooth operation of any organization, including a family. A lack of leadership can cause many problems. As I have allowed my husband the freedom to lead our family, God has blessed us in many ways.

Managing the Children

He must manage his own family well and see that his children obey him with proper respect.

1 Timothy 3:4

Another important part of what your husband manages is the children. This is an area we can react to strongly because of the many fears we can have concerning our children.

Jim was very strict with our sons when it came to issues of safety. He was on the conservative side, and sometimes I felt he was a little too cautious, but I knew it would do great damage to his leadership if I opposed him. Occasionally our sons complained to me that they couldn't do something. I would reaffirm Jim's decision, and I would try to give them a positive perspective about his concern for their safety. As I look back, I think Jim was wise in this. Between our two sons, from mishaps as toddlers to sports injuries, they made over fifteen trips to the emergency room.

There were times when my husband had a hard time connecting with our younger teenage son. As I would try to "help" work out things between them, I would find myself in the middle of their conflicts. I almost always made things worse. I learned to busy myself and walk out of the room when there was tension building between them. Sometimes I would go pray. The more I held my tongue, the better things became. It was less confusing about what the problem was. When I had concerns about something going on between my husband and our children, I would mention my concerns to my husband in private.

On one occasion when there was some tension mounting between the two of them, I walked out of the room and I decided to read for awhile. I fell asleep and after waking, I found Jim in his study laying silently face down on the floor. I asked him if he was sick and he replied, "No, I'm praying." Now, I had never seen my husband pray like this before, so I was curious. I asked him what about, and he said our son. I was encouraged. I wasn't interfering, and Jim was taking it higher. From that day on, I began to see some great changes in their relationship. They occasionally had things to work through, but Jim became much more effective as a father as I stepped back and let him do the fathering by himself.

What happens if your husband makes a decision regarding your children that you don't agree with? Let's say your teenager asks your husband for permission to stay over with a friend on Saturday, and your husband gives his okay. But your teen has a homework project due on Monday that he forgot to mention to Dad. You have a couple of choices. One, you could say to your teenager, "No, you are not going anywhere! You have homework to do this weekend." In that instance, you just vetoed your husband's decision.

Another possible solution is to tell your husband in private that the homework is not complete. (I would suggest this be done in private if you tend to argue with your husband. The last thing your child needs is to watch you argue over parenting decisions.) My children knew that I deferred to their father's decision if there was a difference of opinion. I would mention to my husband that there was something else to consider, or I might look at my son and ask him if he had mentioned his homework.

Your husband can decide if the homework is top priority or not. If he has been trying to help your teenager become more responsible, he may let the teen feel the consequence of putting off the homework. Maybe the teen will receive an incomplete grade or a failing grade, but a more valuable lesson may be learned. Which would be a costlier lesson: 1) a mother who is the boss in the home or 2) a bad grade for a homework assignment?

If your child comes into the room where both you and your husband are sitting and asks for permission to do something, who makes the decision? Do you defer to your husband or do you tend to make the decisions? If you are the one who makes all the decisions regarding the children, ask yourself why? Do you trust your husband's leadership?

It will help set up your husband as leader if you seek his input when your children ask you for permission to do something. There are a couple of ways to do that. One, you could tell your children that you will speak with their father and get back to them. Another way is to send them to their father to make their request. This worked great for our family. One result of this was that Jim often asked me for input before he gave them an answer. We were much more unified. There were times when my husband was out of town or unavailable, so I would make the decision. But if he was available, I preferred that he make the decision. It helped to order the relationships in the home. If I didn't respect their father as the head of our household, it was less likely that our boys would.

I'm not saying that you should never make decisions on what your children do. But if you make all the decisions about what they do, you are hurting their relationship with their father.

The inner strength of a gentle spirit can help you overcome the fears of motherhood. We can give our husbands some valuable input as they make decisions for the family, but it should be done in a respectful way with the understanding that we are there to support and help, not lead or dominate the marriage. Staying out of the dad role and staying in your role will be a great blessing to your children.

Worksheet 19 – Handing over the Management

1. Is your husband the manager of your household?

2. Do you see any areas in which you don't allow him to manage? If so, why? Is it sin or does it go against your personal preferences?

3. Are you afraid of something?

4. Do you second-guess your husband's decisions?

If you have children:

5. Do you frequently interfere with his interactions with them?

6. Who would your children say is the "boss" in your home?

7. Is your marriage a blessing to your children?

8. Write a prayer asking God to guide your husband as he leads your family.

...and to him who knocks, the door will be opened.

Matthew 7:8

Am I a good listener?

Everyone should be quick to listen, slow to speak and slow to become angry.

James 1:19

Being a poor listener can hurt your relationship with your husband. It can keep you from being united with him as he tries to lead. It may discourage him from even trying to lead.

Do you feel like your husband is a reluctant leader in your home? If you do, you need to evaluate your listening habits. If you dominate your conversations with your husband, you may be making it hard for him to lead. When you and your husband are in the same room, which one of you talks the most? It's okay that one spouse talks more than the other. I think that has a lot to do with whom we marry. But if you want your husband to be a stronger leader, you should consider how much you talk. If you talk more than him, I would encourage you to try to draw out your husband in your conversations by being a better listener. Work hard not to dominate your conversations. Develop your listening skills. Consider the following verse:

When words are many, sin is not absent, but he who holds his tongue is wise.

Proverbs 10:19

Do you answer questions for your husband? Letting your husband speak for himself is a great way to grow in respect for him. Consider this verse:

For the husband is the head of the wife as Christ is the head of the church…

Ephesians 5:23

If your husband is the head, he should be allowed to think for himself. Some women are shocked when they realize how often they try to tell their husbands what to think or how to think, or how often they correct him or finish his sentences. If your husband is reluctant to talk very much, the more you respect his ideas, the more open he will be with you about his deepest thoughts. That can bring you closer together.

Being a good listener is one of the sincerest forms of respect that you can show someone, and it can have a positive impact on your marriage.

● – ●

Worksheet 20 - Conversations

1. Are you a good listener?

2. If the two of you are asked a question, who typically answers?

3. Is your husband a reluctant leader? If so, do you generally talk more than him?

4. Do you interrupt your husband, answer for him or finish his sentences? If so, why? What impact does it have on him or your communication?

Do I ask for help?

> *But I am afraid that just as Eve was deceived by the serpent's cunning, your minds may somehow be led astray from your sincere and pure devotion to Christ.*
> *2 Corinthians 11:3*

One lesson we can learn from Eve is to ask for help. Do you get input from your husband before you make decisions? Eve lost the protection of her husband when she made the decision to eat the forbidden fruit.

Jim loves to help me solve my problems, and he is also very objective about my schedule. But it took me years to get to the point where I would ask him for his input. After I came to this new conviction, I asked Jim if he thought it was a good time for me to take an upholstery class offered by the community college. This was something I had been thinking of doing for several years, and it was very appealing to me. But he felt I was too busy and should wait to do it at another time.

I had previously thought through how I would respond if he said no. I wanted to respond righteously. To give you an idea of how far I had to come – early in my marriage, I quit a job without even consulting Jim. I just came home and announced that I gave notice! I was dangerously independent. Like Eve, I lost the protection of my husband when I made independent decisions. Jim told me no regarding the upholstery class the following semester. I let some time go by and asked again. At that time he said it would be great for me to do it. He thought my schedule was under control, and it would be good for me to do something like that.

I appreciate Jim's input on my schedule. Back then I was often overwhelmed with my schedule, because I tried to do too many things. Jim and I would disagree on what I was trying to accomplish. I had a tendency to overbook my schedule. He felt I did things for everyone else and didn't take care of our own family. I would be exhausted by the time he got home because of what I had done earlier in the day. I didn't know when to say no. By the time my family was home from work and school, I had no energy left for them. And when I was exhausted, I would be more apt to get into a disagreement with Jim.

I've learned to get Jim's help on things that I want to do, whether it's for work or fun. He is usually very positive about helping me work through my schedule. If he doesn't want me to do something, I trust his input, even if it is a simple thing like not wanting me to buy groceries late at night. I trust that. Maybe that is how God is protecting me from something.

If someone asks my advice about something, I often ask, "What does your husband think?" A frequent response I've gotten has been, "I didn't ask him." I then encourage her to find out what he thinks she should do and then call me back. One of the greatest things I can teach a younger woman is to seek and rely on her husband's leadership. I want to set her up for success in the relationship in which God has called her to be fully submissive. It will also help her develop a more intimate relationship with him if she relies on his counsel.

One concern I've received from women is, "What if he makes a mistake?" Maybe he will. But is that a reason to disregard the Bible? Don't we all make mistakes?

Once a young wife called me to get some advice. Her husband had already given her his opinion, and I thought it was great advice. She still wanted to know what I thought she should do. I thought she should take her husband's input. She wanted to make sure she was making the most "spiritual" decision, but her turning away from his leadership was unspiritual.

I'm not saying don't get advice from other people, but realize if you are always second-guessing your husband's leadership, it will have a negative impact on your closeness as a couple.

If you are independent, remember Eve. Don't give up the protection of your husband and the joy of letting him help you do something you want to do. Asking for his help will protect you from making poor decisions and help you grow closer in your marriage.

Worksheet 21 – Asking For Help!

1. Are you exhausted by all you try to accomplish?

2. Do you seek your husband's input before you schedule something?

3. Is your schedule a source of conflict with your husband?

Am I quick to make it right when I've been unkind or disrespectful?

> *If you have been trapped by what you said, ensnared by the words of your mouth, then do this, my son, to free yourself, since you have fallen into your neighbor's hands: Go and humble yourself; press your plea with your neighbor! Allow no sleep to your eyes, no slumber to your eyelids. Free yourself, like a gazelle from the hand of the hunter, like a bird from the snare of the fowler.*
>
> Proverbs 6:2-5

Can you easily apologize? If you find that you are being disrespectful to your husband, can you say that you are sorry? Saying, "I'm sorry, that was disrespectful," works great. It will take humility, but remember God gives favor to the humble person (James 4:6). That is why humility is a strength – God is on your side. You will melt your husband's heart, too.

I try to do this on the spot whenever I find I'm being disrespectful. The sooner the better because there is less damage to repair!

● – ●

Worksheet 22 – Making it Right

1. Is it hard for you to apologize?

_____

_____

_____

_____

_____

_____

Am I afraid of something?

> *...like Sarah, who obeyed Abraham and called him her master. You are her daughters if you do what is right and do not give way to fear.*
>
> *1 Peter 3:6*

Next time you are in a disagreement with your husband, ask yourself this question: "Am I afraid of something?" If you can discover any underlying fear, you will be better equipped to know what it is you must overcome. And it may help you discover something new about yourself.

- -

Worksheet 23 – Overcoming Fear

1.   What are your greatest fears?

_____

_____

_____

2.   What motivates you to argue?

_____

_____

_____

_____

_____

_____

Self-Evaluation Summary

Hopefully, these questions have helped you evaluate your level of respect for your husband and how surrendered you are to your role as a wife.

What does it mean to have a gentle and quiet spirit? The following are some of my indicators:

- I'm not bossy or demanding.
- I have control over my emotions.
- I'm peaceful.
- My words are gracious.
- I'm completely surrendered and at peace with my husband's leadership.
- My respect for my husband is obvious.
- I'm not giving in to fear.

Remember that gentleness is a state of mind and heart rather than just actions. If you focus only on your actions, you are missing the point. We are striving for a change of heart that overflows into our relationship with our husbands. Growing in a gentle and quiet spirit is a process, so don't be discouraged – be determined. God will bless you.

-*Chapter 7*-

When It Hurts

Problems in marriage can cause a great deal of pain. What cuts deepest into your heart? Is it hurtful words? Does it hurt if he forgets your birthday? How do you respond when something hurts? Consider the following scenario.

Margie and her husband, Joe, have been married 14 years. They have two children. They lead a small Bible study group, and they coordinate a service program for their congregation at a local children's home. They are well-thought-of, faithful Christians with a strong family. This past weekend Joe and Margie organized a spring cleanup for the children's home. They had planned a day of planting flowers and beautifying the grounds of the home, ending with a barbecue with all the workers and the children from the home. It was a great day. At church services the following day, an announcement was made thanking those who helped. Joe and Margie felt good that they had made a difference.

Margie and Joe are working hard, but what's going on in their marriage? On Friday before the service day, Joe got home from work, ate a quick meal and had to go to his son's soccer game. When he got home and checked his messages, he found he had only twelve of the twenty volunteers needed for the next day's activities. He had forgotten to make an announcement on Sunday, but planned to make a few calls early in the week to get more help. He got busy and before he knew it, the week was over. He was feeling frustrated with himself for not being more organized. Margie walks in and asks Joe to help her load the van with the supplies for the barbecue. Out of his frustration, Joe responds, "Margie, why can't I count on you to do your part?" Ouch! Margie is doing her part. She worked hard to plan the barbecue. The truth is Joe often needs to be more organized and is now taking out his frustration on Margie. What is Margie to do? Let's look at two possible responses.

Response No. 1:

> Margie is deeply hurt by his comment. She is tired of Joe blaming her for his weakness. She leaves the room, slams the door and doesn't speak to him the rest of the night. The next morning she packs the van while Joe is on the phone getting more help. They go to the children's home, work hard, play hard and laugh. At home that night Margie is still silent and sleeps with her back to Joe. Sunday morning when they get up, Joe wants to know why they are out of milk. Margie lets him have it. She calls him a jerk and says, "If you want milk, go get it yourself. You don't appreciate anything I do for you!"

Response No. 2:

> Margie is deeply hurt by his comment. She responds, "Ouch." She walks out of the room and goes to the back porch to pray a few minutes. She asks God for strength. She tucks the kids in bed, finishes her work and goes to bed. The next morning she asks Joe if everything is okay. He answers, "I have only 12 people coming today." Margie asks, "Is there anything I can do to help?" Joe is feeling very guilty about his harshness and he responds, "Why are you so good to me? I'm sorry about last night. Will you forgive me?" She says yes. Then they go do the work and enjoy their day together.

Consider Margie's purity and reverence in these two responses. It would take a strong woman with a gentle and quiet spirit to respond in the second way. Look at the difference in the outcome. When Margie was gracious, compassionate and kind to her husband, even though his weakness was a hardship on her, she was able to get the situation turned around. She offered her help, but didn't take over her husband's leadership. She let him work through his own issue without making it a bigger issue that affected much more of their relationship.

I made up this story, but the responses are very similar to ways I've responded to my husband in the past and his response to me. I've responded in the wrong way and the right way, and I've seen the fruit of both. Before I did it the right way, I had no idea there was this kind of influence available to me. I thought I needed to stand up for my rights and not put up with anything ungodly from my husband. I wasted a lot of precious energy and time.

If you are a mom, you should also consider how this would affect your children. You may think they don't know what's going on, but they do. They are very in tune with their parents. Even if you don't fight in front of them, they can see and feel the void of happiness and know something unpleasant is going on.

There are many other possible variations to these two responses. In the first response, Margie could be silent for days, because she is holding out for an apology for Joe's insensitive words. The fight could escalate until the word divorce is mentioned and other threats made. This could be one of many situations where there is so much hurt on both sides that it's hard to unravel. Margie could tuck this away and forget about it until the next time Joe is insensitive. Maybe in the second response, Joe doesn't apologize so quickly. Maybe he feels guilty but is too prideful to apologize. Margie may need to dig deep to forgive and not count this against Joe. It may take Joe awhile to change his heart, even if Margie is pure and reverent in her response to him.

How do you handle the pain of your relationship with your husband? Are you an emotional bully who makes his life tough until he comes around? Are you the victim who can't climb out of the hole you feel you've been put in? Are you emotionally beat up because you have little self-control over your own words? Do you give free rein to your emotions? By "free rein" I mean no restraint. If you give free rein to a horse that you are riding, that means you have no control over where he goes. I've accidentally dropped the reins on a horse's bridle, and the only thing I had to hold onto was the horse's mane until I was willing to jump off. It was frightening. Having no control over your emotions is frightening too.

One result of the pain we feel is to respond in a sinful way. Jesus wants us to know we have options and don't have to sin. We can be like him. Let's look at Jesus' example:

> To this you were called, because Christ suffered for you, leaving you an example, that you should follow in his steps. "He committed no sin, and no deceit was found in his mouth." When they hurled their insults at him, he did not retaliate; when he suffered, he made no threats. Instead, he entrusted himself to him who judges justly. He himself bore our sins in his body on the tree, so that we might die to sins and live for righteousness; by his wounds you have been healed.
>
> *1 Peter 2:21-24*

"...he entrusted himself to God"

That means he trusted God. He knew God was working in his life, directing his life and also working in the lives of the people who were mistreating him. Some of these people later became Christians.

"He committed no sin, and no deceit was found in his mouth."

He carefully guarded his tongue. Nothing unrighteous or deceitful came out of his mouth. Deceitfulness is an attempt to avoid suffering. I have sinned by shading the truth so that my husband wouldn't be upset about something I did. Deceitfulness will create barriers to your closeness as a couple.

Another way we can be deceitful is to exaggerate the truth by twisting our husbands' words. We can take the words he says and, in our insecurity or bitterness, draw a damaging conclusion. There have been many times when a friend has told me something that her husband said, and

I later heard her say, "Well, it wasn't exactly what he said, but it's what he meant!" There is no benefit to exaggeration. Deceit is a dangerous sin, and one of Satan's most effective tools. Follow Jesus' example of honesty.

"…no threats"

There are many ways we can threaten our husbands. "I'm withdrawing my love from you. I'm never going to bring up anything ever again! I'm not putting up with you anymore! I'm moving out! I'm going to divorce you!" All threats.

"…did not retaliate"

Retaliation goes a little further than a threat. It's repaying evil with evil. "Since you bought things not in the budget, I did too. I said unkind words to you because you said them to me. Because you hurt my feelings, I haven't talked to you for days."

Jesus did not sin, threaten or retaliate. He chose to please God rather than sin in response to someone's unkind or evil actions toward him.

"by his wounds you have been healed"

His wounds are the key for us to overcome the pain of our own wounds. We must remember what God has done for us. Luke 6:35 says that God is kind to the ungrateful and wicked. That includes you and me. His kindness led us to repentance (Romans 2:4). He loved us and was kind to us before we knew we needed him (Romans 5:8-11).

Have you let your past wounds be healed by the cross? Consider any unresolved issues you may have in your marriage and look at them in light of the cross. The cross gives us a new perspective. It doesn't mean there won't be a scar. A wound may leave a scar, but it's not bleeding anymore. It's healed. Jesus makes up the difference by his incredible love and mercy.

If you don't feel healed, you may need to better understand the cross and the love shown you by God. Maybe you have forgotten or maybe you need to go deeper into the scriptures. You and I don't deserve what God has given us. There are several scriptures leading up to this in 1 Peter that are reminders of this great gift of mercy.

Praise be to the God and Father of our Lord Jesus Christ! In his great mercy he has given us new birth into a living hope through the resurrection of Jesus Christ from the dead, and into an inheritance that can never perish, spoil or fade—kept in heaven for you,

1 Peter 1:3-4

For you know that it was not with perishable things such as silver or gold that you were redeemed from the empty way of life handed down to you from your forefathers, but with the precious blood of Christ, a lamb without blemish or defect.

1 Peter 1:18-19

But you are a chosen people, a royal priesthood, a holy nation, a people belonging to God, that you may declare the praises of him who called you out of darkness into his wonderful light. Once you were not a people, but now you are the people of God; once you had not received mercy, but now you have received mercy.

1 Peter 2:9-10

Consider how you respond when you are hurt. If you sin in response to being hurt and then justify your sin, you have lost sight of the mercy and forgiveness shown you at the cross. Jesus gave us an example to follow, and he expects us to follow in his footsteps – no threats, no retaliation, no sin and no deceit. This is a high calling, isn't it? God is *not* trying to make our life tough – he wants to bless us.

Immediately after 1 Peter 2:21-25 about responding righteously like Jesus to our challenges, he mentions the marriage relationship. 1 Peter 3:1 begins, "Wives, in the same way…" Then in verse 7, he says, "Husbands, in the same way…" In the same way that Jesus trusted God and responded righteously to his challenges, husbands and wives are to follow his example. (I can't think of a more appropriate and practical application of how to put 1 Peter 2:21-25 into practice.) Then immediately after this instruction to husbands and wives, he states the following:

Do not repay evil with evil or insult with insult, but with blessing, because to this you were called so that you may inherit a blessing. For, "Whoever would love life and see good days must keep his tongue from evil and his lips from deceitful speech. He must turn from evil and do good; he must seek peace and pursue it. For the eyes of the Lord are on the righteous and his ears are attentive to their prayer, but the face of the Lord is against those who do evil."

1 Peter 3:9-12

God wants to bless you with a great marriage. He has great plans for your life, but you must be willing to suffer in a righteous way. Suffering produces something good in us. Longsuffering is actually a fruit of the Spirit.

Longsuffering

But the fruit of the Spirit is love, joy, peace, patience [makrothumia], kindness, goodness, faithfulness, gentleness and self-control.

Galatians 5:22-23

The Greek word translated "patience" in this verse is *makrothumia*

Definition: *Makrothumia*, (mak-roth-oo-mee'-ah) fortitude, longsuffering, patience.[23]

This word means longsuffering – being able to suffer long. Why would that be a fruit? It doesn't sound very sweet to me. I think of fruits of the Spirit as being something sweet, such as love, joy and peace. Maybe patience or longsuffering is like the lemon! The lemon has no sugar in it, but lemons can make a big difference with the other fruits. When I make a fruit salad, I squeeze a little lemon juice on it to keep it from turning dark. It has a purpose. Our suffering has a purpose too. Suffering produces perseverance, character and hope. (Romans 5:3-5)

(In this discussion, I am not addressing abusive behavior. Please reread the section on "Fear of Abuse" if you are in an abusive relationship.)

1 Peter 2:20 says, "But how is it to your credit if you receive a beating for doing wrong and endure it? But if you suffer for doing good and you endure it, this is commendable before God." Many of the emotional hurts that I've endured in my relationship with my husband would have been avoided if I had known how to have a gentle and quiet (*praus* and *hesuchios*) spirit. I brought on a great deal of my own suffering, because I

134

was out of my role as a wife and was being disrespectful to my husband. There have been a few times I didn't deserve a bad attitude or some kind of negative response from Jim, but God still wants me to have a godly response even in those situations.

One tool that has helped me work through some of my hurts is the question, "What would a humble woman do?" Now, since I'm not a humble woman, I have no idea! I have to imagine it! But it is a good question for me. A humble woman would not be offended. A humble woman would not be bitter either. I've also found that gracious speech solves a lot of the challenges I face.

Jesus gave us an example of a righteous response. He surrendered himself to God's plan for his life. He also showed us incredible love by his sacrifice. There are great blessings by following Jesus' example of a righteous response.

Worksheet 24 – A Righteous Response

1. If you sin against your husband, do you take responsibility for it or pass the blame?

2. Do you retaliate when you are hurt?

3. Do you ever make threats?

4. Write a prayer asking God to help you have a righteous response when you are hurt.

If you remain in me and my words remain in you, ask whatever you wish, and it will be given you. — John 15:7

- Chapter 8-

Happily Ever After

God can help each one of us improve our marriage. He can help turn around a troubled marriage and get it back on track. He can help an okay marriage become a great marriage. He can help a marriage of many years experience new growth.

Hopefully, your best years are ahead of you – not behind you. I have been married over 30 years. I love my marriage, but I still want to see my relationship with my husband grow. I want to live "happily ever after."

If you are in the middle of problems, remember that God can help you. I like to put my problems in perspective by thinking through the problems God solved in the Bible. He parted the Red Sea even though that looked impossible. He gave his people victories in battles over vast armies.

One of my favorite Old Testament passages is Joshua 6:1-2 where the Israelites crossed over into the Promised Land and marched to the city of Jericho. Jericho was shut up tightly. God said to Joshua, "See I have delivered Jericho into your hands, along with its king and its fighting men." Joshua might not have seen it that way initially, because Jericho was one of the most fortified cities of that time. The Israelites were not an accomplished army. They were nomads who had just come into a new land. Only by faith could Joshua look at this city and think that it was already his.

You may see your marriage like the city of Jericho – a fortified city that looks impossible to conquer. But that is not how God sees it. He wants to bless you with a great marriage. You can accomplish this by following what he has set out for you to do. God has empowered us as wives. We can have an incredible influence with our husbands when we follow the Bible.

We can also find help through our relationships in the church. One of the greatest treasures we have in the church is having close "sister" relationships. What a blessing to have a friend who will take time to help. We sometimes need the fresh perspective of a friend – her faith and inspiration. If you are a newlywed, praise God for older women paving the way for you to have a better marriage. If you are an oldlywed (like Sarah), dig deep and go after some great changes in your marriage. You are never too old to enjoy a close, intimate relationship with your husband.

Remember that we have lofty goals and if we miss, God is merciful. We will always be growing in our marriages – from "I do" through our retirement and into the nursing home. It's part of the adventure of life, and we glorify God as we face our new challenges with faith.

The older I become and the longer I am married, the more I see my need for my husband's help and input and the more I appreciate his leadership and protection. What an incredible blessing my husband is to me. I cringe when I think of how independent I was when I was younger and how deceived I was to my real situation. God has blessed my marriage in ways I could not even dream of. I have an incredible friendship with my husband, and I feel honored to be led by such a spiritual man. He isn't perfect, but neither am I! I trust Jim to lead, and I trust God to help him be successful.

As I strive to live a pure and reverent life, God helps me discern what is in my heart. I still see my role as a submissive and surrendered wife as a high calling, and I deeply appreciate the forgiveness and grace that

God lavishes on me (Ephesians 1:7-8). When I'm not joyful, I search out my heart. Sometimes I just need to let go of something that is not mine to control, and then turn it over to God and trust him to take care of it.

A Gentle And Quiet Spirit

A woman with a gentle and quiet spirit is a woman of strength and peace. She is surrendered to God, and she willingly submits to the leadership of her husband. She considers her own motives to make sure she is pure-hearted. Knowing that God understands her deepest thoughts and feelings, she strives to please him above all else, even when it is difficult. She speaks with gracious and wise words and has a powerful influence on her husband, and her life overflows with tranquillity.

I encourage you to reread the first part of this book when you need strength. I have had to saturate myself with the study of reverence and purity to help me repent of my independence, overcome my fears, and surrender to my husband's leadership. Let's overcome our fears and become daughters of Sarah, and to God be the glory!

Worksheet 25 – Don't Give Up

1. How has God already blessed your marriage?

2. Read Luke 18:1 and Galatians 6:9. If you don't get quick results, do you give up? When are you most likely to give up?

3. Write a prayer asking God to help you not give up in any way as you develop a gentle and quiet spirit?

Then Jesus told his disciples a parable to show them that they should always pray and not give up. — Luke 18:1

ENDNOTES:

---

1 W. E. Vine, *Vine's Expository Dictionary of Old and New Testament Words* (Tarrytown, NY: Fleming H. Revell Company, 1981).

2 Ibid.

3 Ibid.

4 Ibid.

5 Ibid.

6 James Strong, *Strong's Exhaustive Concordance* (Nashville, TN: Crusade Bible Publishers, Inc.).

7 Vine.

8 Ibid.

9 Strong.

10 John Gray, Ph.D., *Men Are From Mars, Women Are From Venus* (New York, NY: Harper Collins, 1992), p. 15.

11 Strong.

12 Vine.

13 Strong.

14 Ibid.

15 Erma Bombeck, *A Marriage Made in Heaven or Too Tired for an Affair* (New York, NY: Harper Collins, 1993), pp. 6-7.

16 Strong.

17 John Eldredge, *Wild at Heart* (Nashville, TN: Thomas Nelson Publishers, 2001), p. 51.

18 Robert Lewis and William Hendricks, *Rocking the Roles* (Colorado Springs, CO: Navpress, 1991), p. 99.

19 Strong.

20 Gray, p. 21.

21 Strong.

22 Vine.

23 Strong.

Pursuing Purity

Protection, Power and Peace
for Every Christian Woman

By Virginia Lefler

In a world of declining standards, purity is seldom honored or pursued. In fact, many women believe that a worldly woman is strong and secure while a woman who strives for purity and strength from God is naïve and vulnerable. Nothing could be further from the truth. A worldly woman is more hardened than strong and her security depends mostly on the day's events. To find real strength and be secure in our world, we must know and embrace God's timeless standards for purity.

Pursuing Purity offers hope and solutions. Discover the protection, power and peace that God promises to those who purify themselves. Worksheets throughout the book make it especially useful as a personal or group study guide.

THE COMPLETE
GUIDE *to* GRACE

By James L. Lefler

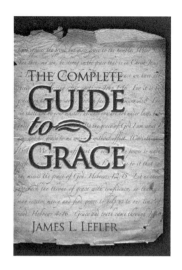

A clear understanding of God's grace is empowering, but explanations of grace often do more to muddy the water than clarify the meaning. The words grace, mercy and salvation are used interchangeably in ways inconsistent with the original Hebrew and Greek. Frequently grace is defined as unmerited favor; however, when we focus on how unworthy we are to receive it, we make it more about us than about God and risk missing the full impact of his favor.

The Complete Guide to Grace is a refreshing, motivating and comprehensive study that clears up misconceptions about grace. It reveals foundational truths about grace, mercy and forgiveness that can radically change your life. It will help you discover for yourself what Abraham discovered about grace, faith and obedience. Worksheets throughout the book make it useful as a personal or group study guide.

BOOKS AND TEACHING AIDS ARE AVAILABLE AT:

SilverdayPress.com